The Shadow Knows:

Uncovering and Integrating the Shadow

Mickey Eliason

DEDICATION

This book is dedicated to the memory of Angeles Arrien, who passed from this earth in April of 2014 but who lives on in the lives of the countless people she touched through her writing, lectures, and teaching.

CONTENTS

ACKNOWLEDGMENTS

The seed for this book really began to germinate several years ago, while I was pondering my life as a student in Angeles Arrien's personal growth/spirituality classes. This exposure to a masterful teacher over an 11-year period in the many workshops and classes she offered was a profound experience. I owe a huge debt of gratitude to Angeles for teaching me so many valuable life lessons, many of which I have been exploring in my own writing since her death in 2014. In addition to Angeles, I wish to thank the FourFold Way™ group that has been meeting twice a month for more than four years to continue the work we all started with Angeles. Over the years, we have often done shadow work, whether we called it that or not. That group includes Meigs Matheson, Louis Rosenbaum, Pat Usner, Marcia Branca, Tekla Cohn, Julie Lavezzo, Gaye Raymond, and Sarah Cane. Our discussions have helped me to clarify how all these complex psychological mechanisms might work and how they fit into Angeles' work. This group offers much support for the hard work of befriending the shadow. In the years that we have been meeting regularly, they have graciously allowed me to try out activities and ideas with them and always have great feedback. Thank you all for your willingness to be vulnerable and commit to this work.

1 INTRODUCTION

"The shadow is simply a mythological name for all that within me of which I cannot know" Marie Louis von Franz

"To contemplate is to look at shadows" Victor Hugo

Bad behavior seems the norm these days in our divided nation, where some commentators even suggest that we are close to "civil war" in the U.S. We seem to have a crisis in communication, and civil debate about issues is growing ever more difficult in our polarized world. We have far too much "childish" behavior, such as taunting and name-calling and blaming others, from our so-called leaders. The world clearly needs more adults who behave ethically and responsibly. But how do we become fully actualized and mature adults, not driven by petty fears, doubts, and irrational behaviors? In this current political climate of greed, environmental degradation, and distrust/hatred of other people, what can we do to make this world a better place? Like so many of my friends and acquaintances, I spend much of my time these days in angst over what actions I can take that might make a difference. When that angst gets too great, I return to what I learned from Angeles Arrien. She always said that the one thing we are all capable of doing is the self-work that makes us more authentic and strengthens our moral compass. If enough of us do that kind of work, collectively we can and will change the course of history. When in doubt about how to make changes in our lives, Angeles recommended that we "tool up." That is, she suggested that we go out and learn the skills we need to tackle the issue and get to work on ourselves. Find your "growing edge," she said; that place just outside of the comfort zone.

The type of personal work that most of us desperately need is to identify and integrate the shadow aspects into our conscious awareness. We cannot feel whole until we acknowledge all aspects of ourselves and befriend the parts that scare us or do not fit our self-image--the parts that we have repressed and denied for most of our lifetimes. This book will delve into ideas of the shadow that come from many different sources and focus on practical exercises designed to identify those hard-to-see shadow aspects of our selves so that they do not drive our behavior without our knowledge. This is a workbook—the shadow cannot be addressed by reading and thinking about it alone. It requires some digging through the depths of the conscious mind and then going deeper into the unconscious. Some of our shadow is buried pretty deep, so we need some big excavation tools. Get out the shovel or start up the backhoe and prepare to get dirty! The focus in this book is on the practices, and the theoretical background information will be kept to a minimum. Interested readers can refer to the 'Works Cited' page for resource materials that go into more depth on the theory of the shadow.

Why Do Shadow Work Now?

It's hard not to feel despair when confronted with the current national and global climate of hatred, distrust, war, climate change, and corporate greed. I so often find myself lapsing into a sense of helplessness that can be paralyzing. I have marched in protests, signed petitions, written letters and called politicians, watched the news obsessively, and talked to friends about my feelings—and they all seem to share that hopelessness. It feels like we can never do enough, that our actions do not actually accomplish anything. Then I picked up Carl Jung's *The Undiscovered Self*, written in 1957, and it seemed that the world was almost exactly the same then as it is now. Jung was writing about post-World War II Europe and focusing mostly on eastern European dictatorships. He noted that when people mass together in a "State" with collective goals, and are no longer are dependent on values of the individual, "to compensate for its chaotic formlessness, a mass always produces a 'Leader' who infallibly becomes the victim of his own inflated ego-consciousness" (p. 9). At the time of this writing, we have a president with a vastly over-inflated ego; one who acts like a narcissistic school yard bully. We do not have an adult at the helm. We have a man who projects his shadow onto the world stage for all to see.

And, Jung continued, when the Church and State merge as they have over the past few years in the U.S, the religious component, which was originally about an individual's personal relationship with God or a path of salvation or enlightenment, devolves into a "creed." A creed is a social contract with no moral foundation, so "the State takes the place of God; that is why…the socialist dictatorships are religious and State slavery is a form of worship" (p. 15). Jung thought that this State/religion merged entity raises "secret doubts" among the people, which are repressed to avoid conflict, but those repressed doubts turn into an overcompensation in the form of fanaticism "which in turn is used as a weapon for stamping out the least flicker of opposition" (p. 15). Sound familiar? Although Jung was writing mostly about Eastern Europe at that time, he noted that the United States was particularly vulnerable to this type of State dictatorship for two reasons. First, our educational system is so based on science, with its abstract generalizations and theories about human behavior that make the unique individual and their personal moral and spiritual development disappear. Second, because the diverse immigrants who live here often cannot find a historical home that feels safe and inclusive in the U.S. Immigrants become disenfranchised and demonized. We are a house divided against itself.

The strategies that Jung noted were at play to maintain State power still ring true today—"even a dictator thinks it necessary not only to accompany his acts of State with threats but to stage them with all manner of solemnities. Brass bands, flags, banners, parades..." (p. 16). To keep the masses in line, he noted "If religion requires the 'fear of God' then the dictator State takes good care to provide the necessary terror" (p. 16). Another weapon of the State is to lie to the people and Jung wrote "the ethical decision of the individual human being no longer counts—what alone matters is the blind movement of the masses, and the lie thus becomes the operative principle of political action" (p. 17). In a more contemporary example, Parker Palmer (2018) suggested that the shadow is behind much of the anti-immigrant sentiment that the world is experiencing today. He noted "some consequences [of the shadow] are political, and when people who fear what feels alien in themselves project their fear on the 'alien other'— while shameless politicians cynically manipulate that fear as they play the dangerous divide and conquer game" we all lose.

In this grim reality, what solutions did Jung offer? Only one, and the same one as Angeles Arrien suggested: "the salvation of the world consists in the salvation of the individual soul" (p. 32). We have to reclaim our moral compass, and to do that and move toward wholeness, we have to integrate each aspect of the shadow, as it emerges into view, into our psyche or self. Only then will we truly have the skills and maturity to shape the external world.

Even if the world was not in the uncertain and hateful state of affairs that we find ourselves in today, we would still need to do the inner work of reincorporating our shadow. We cannot fully eradicate the hate, anger, greed, and competition that lead to violence if we do not address the destructive tendencies within ourselves. And we cannot lead authentic lives without dealing with the shadow. Jung said

> Yearning is the way of life. If you do not acknowledge your yearning, then you do not follow yourself, but go on foreign ways that others have indicated to you. So you do not live your life but an alien one...It is not only stupid to exchange your life for an alien one, but also a hypocritical game because you can never really live the life of others, you can only pretend to do it, deceiving the other and yourself" (2009, p. 188).

Many of us have repressed our yearnings as well as other manifestations of the shadow, and have to rediscover what is important to us. We have to re-imagine our life purpose at some point in our lives. The journey is not easy. As David Richo (1999) noted, our egos, the part of our conscious mind that protects us from real and perceived threats, will resist spiritual growth work, because this type of work requires us to give up control, revenge and entitlement. I mean, really, who wants to give these up? We use these immature impulses to avoid feeling vulnerable. But consider how the world would change if everyone gave up just a little of these destructive impulses? We can be the frontrunners of a movement to set a better example for the next generation. To experience ourselves as whole and live in our full integrity, we must release these damaging tendencies. Parker Palmer (2018) in his latest book about aging noted that "the unexamined life is a threat to others." Shadow work is not only for our own edification, but for other people around us as well. Like Angeles, Palmer thought that "violence is what happens when we don't know what to do with our suffering."

Connie Zweig and Steve Wolf (1997) listed several positive outcomes that result from doing shadow work. A few of them include an increase in self-love and self-acceptance, better family relationships, the breaking of old destructive family patterns, increased capacity for intimacy, increased sense of authenticity, and a heightened capacity to re-imagine our life purpose. The work will reap many positive benefits, so let's get started!

The Influence of Angeles Arrien on Shadow Work

I owe my interest in the shadow to Angeles Arrien. Even though my undergraduate and graduate degrees were in psychology, I had heard only passing reference to Jung in any of my classes and had never heard of the psychological shadow before I started working with Angeles when I was in my early 50s. I went to school in the heyday of the cognitive behavioral movement and thinkers like Jung were disdained as historic relics. Jung in particular was dismissed as a "mystic" or a bit of a kook, and not a real scientist. Angeles was influenced by Jung but developed her own take on concepts like the shadow and archetypes. Her program was rooted in the wisdom of the indigenous peoples of the world, whereas Jung and other western psychologists were more heavily influenced by the western world of science and European perennial wisdom and philosophy. I found this blending of indigenous and western thought to be more relevant to my own life than either separately.

Angeles often referred to the shadow in her personal growth programs, workshops, and books, the *Fourfold Way*™ and the *Second Half of Life* most notably, as well as in all of her classes. The *FourFold Way*™ is based on four archetypes, or major types of roles/contributions that people make to the world that are found in every indigenous culture: The Warrior (leader); the Healer; the Visionary; and the Teacher. We all carry all four archetypes in ourselves, but often only express one or two of them and leave the others underdeveloped. Angeles explained that for every archetype's positive qualities (courage, patience, nonattachment, love, authenticity, wisdom, vision, etc.), over-identification with an archetype could lead to the shadow emerging and taking over. For everything illuminated by the light, a problem could be lurking in the shadow cast by that trait. Angeles also noted that many of us have positive qualities that are obscured by the shadow. We don't see them, so we cannot tap into their potential. In Angeles' perspective the psychological shadow is not the answer to the old radio show opener: "What evil lurks in the hearts of men? The Shadow knows." The shadow contains evil, it's true, and all the bad qualities that we would rather not own up to, like impatience, greed, judgmental thinking, a desire to control, aggression. It also includes good qualities that we buried inside of us and never let blossom, like artistic abilities, leadership skills, patience, and courage. It includes memories and capabilities that we have forgotten with the passage of time and unresolved old issues; information that could be helpful to us now. Fear keeps us from acknowledging these old wounds and repressed traits. When we do not acknowledge the shadow, those unexpressed aspects of our true selves start to fester and cause problems in our lives. This is particularly true as we reach our second half of life. At some point, we need to become whole again. To do this, we have to take Rumi's advice and "Do not move the way fear wants you to."

All of us who choose to follow a contemplative path in life and reflect on our experiences will encounter the shadow. It emerges in all types of spiritual or personal growth work and is part of our maturation processes. We can work on the shadow in a number of ways, through work with a mentor/teacher, through rigorous self-examination and daily practices, through journaling, meditation, dream work, drumming meditations, journey work, or working with a therapist or other type of healer. We need to establish a regular practice, because shadow work is ongoing for the rest of our lives.

The Origins of This Book

Every summer since I started working with Angeles, I wrote a short story that summarized the seeds of my learning for that year. After Angeles' death, I felt a need to step up my work to further understand her teaching and integrate it more into my daily life. I've done bigger, meatier projects each year. In 2016, I re-organized all of my notes (from 13 journals spanning an 11-year period) into a book format that deepened and strengthened my learning and I self-published it for others who wanted an encyclopedia format of terms and concepts that Angeles used extensively in her work (Eliason, 2016). So much of Angeles' own work had deepened and evolved from the time she wrote the *FourFold Way* in 1993 that had not been written down. One topic that came up often was shadow work. During the last year of working with Angeles, I picked up a new blank journal off of a sale table at a book store. The front cover depicted the Wicked Witch of the West, a character with whom I have had a fascination for years. She's pretty scary, but there's something kind of cool about her at the same time. She was a powerful woman, at least until she was taken down by a lowly teenager from Kansas who learned to integrate her shadow and become whole. As a child, I was both afraid and fascinated by her, a phenomenon I know now is defined as sublime (fascination tinged with terror). I recognize her as a symbol of my shadow side. I try to project an image as a kind and compassionate person, but I've got an inner wicked witch to contend with. I wrote on the first page of the journal that this would be my shadow work journal. Then I set it aside for four years. On occasion, when I saw it on the stack of unopened journals, I would think, *it's time to do shadow work*. But I quickly and conveniently forgot about it.

Angeles often said that the cusp between the seasons (approximately two weeks before and two weeks after the change of a season) was a time of high creativity and integration work. In 2017, right at the cusp between spring and summer, the need for shadow work seized me in a more urgent fashion. Spring is a time of focus on healing. Summer is a good time for shadow work, Angeles said, because this time of the year is focused on the archetype of the visionary and reclaiming our authentic selves and lost pieces of ourselves. Therefore, the cusp between spring and summer is about healing by reclaiming shadow aspects of the self.

I had been in a difficult situation that helped me glimpse a shadow and it was working me. I started using the Wicked Witch journal and I wrote a 12-page essay of my initial thoughts about the shadow. I put it aside at the end of the summer because of an intensification of my work role. I had the beginnings of a roadmap now but had not yet embarked on the journey. In the spring of 2018, the urge to work on it further returned, and I took up the essay again. I needed answers to some burning questions in my own life. What pieces of myself did I give up in my first half of life that I could now reclaim? Where are those lost pieces of myself that I gave away to appease parents, teachers, religion, or my workplace or community's expectations of me? If the shadow is in the unconscious mind, how do I access it? Once I find the shadow, how do I go about befriending it? But really, why would I even want it as a friend? As the old saying goes, with friends like this, who needs enemies? But eventually, I came to the place of understanding that those shadows could become friends if I extended compassion to myself. As Angeles always pointed out, things are not either/or; they are both/and. I can be brave and fearful at the same time, I can hold both good and evil inside myself; I can be judgmental and compassionate.

The "bad" makes the good possible.

As I contemplated on those questions and started some reflective reading, I realized that we do not need to go on an epic journey abroad to find the shadow. No passports or inoculations or currency exchanges are needed. Most of the time, the shadow qualities are deep inside of ourselves, just out of reach of our conscious mind. Other times, we are dimly aware of them because they have emerged to cause pain, shame, or disappointment in ourselves, but we try to deny or repress them because they are too scary to face head on. Periodically, something calls us to work on shadow aspects or brings them up to the light of day; the season of the visionary, individuation phases (a term that Carl Jung coined for times of intense self-work toward wholeness), dreams, projections, and living to be over the age of 50 are prime examples of motivators to do shadow work. When we reach a point where we care less about what others think of us, we are freed up to face our own demons. All of these motivators call on us to work on the descent/ascent process of shadow work (Arrien, 2005).

I think my impetus for working on this book came from an impending transition—I turned 65 this year and am launching into phased retirement soon. This transition has prompted the need to do shadow work as part of my search for who I am beyond my work identity. How will I find meaning in my life when I leave behind the work I have done for so many years, and that defined me as a person? So, I transformed the original essay into this practical workbook in a furious few months of intensive reading and reflection. I need the structure of specific questions and activities to do deeper work—a blank journal just doesn't do it for me. Writing is a key way of delving into my own shadow if I have the right prompts. I learned from Angeles that personal growth comes from finding the right questions and knowing that the answers would not come easily, or maybe not at all. It's the questions themselves that are important. "Live the questions" Rilke said. Angeles also advised us to "sit with" the questions until some insights arose. I hope that some of the methods I have borrowed from others or worked out to deal with the shadow in myself help others as well—perhaps some of the questions will resonate with you.

Organization of This Book

We have all had very different life experiences, as well as have come from diverse family and cultural backgrounds that contribute to this bag of burdens that we drag along behind us in life. But we also share many of the same shadow qualities, as they are universal human feelings, survival instincts, and common fears and compensatory behaviors.

This book provides some background on the definitions of shadow in common use as well as in psychological theory and spiritual growth literature, but I did not want to overload readers with too much theory. I do devote considerable time and space to the work of Angeles Arrien, since it was her inspiration that brought me to shadow work. The bulk of the workbook contains the reflective practices for addressing shadow in our daily lives. I recommend that you keep a journal of this work. If you like, there is a workbook version of this book with a spiral binding so that it lays flat for easy writing and it has lots of blank pages to record your own experience working through the shadow. It's available from www.lulu.com. Whether you choose the workbook or start your own journal, do write about symbols, dreams, thoughts, and feelings that arise as you do this work. It might be productive to engage intentionally in shadow work at least once a year—the issues that come up as you do these exercises are likely to be different over time, because our life circumstances and our inner challenges change. Let's face it, there is a lifetime's accumulation of material in the shadow, so it will be ongoing work. You don't have to worry about running out of shadow material. It is truly in abundance!

This is not the type of book that you read from cover to cover in one sitting. Instead, I recommend that you read the background information, and then embark on the exercises a few at a time. Ideally, you would do no more than one practice a week, giving yourself time to reflect on the topics and integrate your new learnings. You can do the exercises in any order, although I have tried to order the activities to start with the more superficial shadow qualities and build to deeper work that focuses on integration.

Finally, I recommend that you follow one key principle that Angeles emphasized in her programs: Stay attached to your funny bone. She always said that where you lose your sense of humor, it is a sign that you have become attached to some outcome. So, let go of attachments, and bring your funny bone into this work. When you think about it, the way that our shadow side manipulates us into childish behaviors is pretty funny. Sometimes we act like puppets on a string, controlled by the forces we are afraid to look at. If we are going to act like children, we may as well bring some play into this work! At one point in his adulthood, Jung felt stymied in understanding his own mind. He thought about an activity that he had loved as a child—building structures out of stone and mud. So, he began spending all of his free time building a miniature village. He was also a major doodler! The cultivation of play opened him up to new insights (Jung, 1961). If you feel yourself going all deadly serious and indignant about something in this book or your work with the shadow, take a moment to see if you can spot the attachment or go outside and play!

Preparing for Shadow Work

Let's start with a reflection exercise now. What brings you to shadow work at this time?

***

What have you learned thus far about the impact of the shadow side of your personality? What is your personal understanding or definition of shadow?

***

Have you perceived any problems in your life because of shadow aspects?

***

Have you done any shadow work in the past? How has that gone for you? What feelings do you have about starting this work; fear, excitement, joy, anxiety, or others?

***

What is the most ridiculous thing that your shadow has caused you to do in the past? Exaggerate it into a funny story. If you can laugh at yourself, there's hope!

2 COMMON USES OF SHADOW

"I have a little shadow that goes in and out with me, and what can be the use of him is more than I can see." Robert Louis Stevenson

The next three chapters explore the concept of the shadow from three perspectives. The first perspective includes all the common usages of the word, drawn from dictionary definitions and word origins. Then we will explore how psychologists and philosophers have used the concept in a specific way to describe undesirable or unacknowledged and often unconscious traits or characteristics that we have but of which we are not fully aware. Finally, Angeles Arrien's teachings about shadow are described.

What is the Shadow? Everyday Definitions

Why did Jung choose the word "shadow" to describe unacknowledged qualities of human beings? This concept of psychological shadow seems to differ quite dramatically from the common uses of the word, so we will start with those common usages and try to track them to the more psychological meanings of the word. Nature metaphors are often a helpful way to approach human growth, so even the common understandings of the word shadow may be a helpful starting place as they are rooted in our daily experience. The Oxford dictionary defines the word shadow as both a noun and a verb. As a noun, shadow can mean:

- *A dark area or shape produced by a body coming between rays of light and a surface.* This is the tangible definition of the visual image we can see when something blocks the sun. Metaphorically, perhaps the body that obscures the light in this definition could be our ego, or at least the defense mechanisms that protect our egos, that gets between the light source (our authentic self) and the surface (our lived reality).

- *A word used in reference to proximity, ominous oppressiveness, or sadness and gloom.* This definition resonates with many common uses of the word to connote the "dark side of the force" or the unknown. "Who knows what evil lurks in the hearts of men? The Shadow knows." Shadow is a place of darkness and danger. Indeed, shadow work is risky, because it can totally alter our sense of ourselves. We have to leave our comfort zone to do shadow work.
    - Visualize your comfort zone by imagining it is a physical place. What does it look like? What does the world outside its windows look like? If so inclined, consider drawing a picture of your comfort zone.
- *Something fleeting or insubstantial,* as in "a shadow of her former self" or a ghostly apparition in the darkness. It's often intangible and hard to pin down. That's the first glimpse of shadow that we get—it's out of the corner of the eye, a ghostly haunting, a hint of something there, but not yet clear. It's easy to ignore or dismiss.
- *A small amount,* as in "a shadow of a doubt." It does not take much doubt to set off the suspicious critical mind that creates all violence in the world, as Angeles always said. We may also doubt or resist acknowledging our shadow side, because it's largely hidden from our rational brains. The concept of the unconscious mind is rather daunting—the unconscious pops up in such small glimpses of fleeting ideas in the corner of one's mind. The shadow or hint of an unacknowledged aspect of ourselves is all we get most of the time.
- *An inseparable attendant or companion,* as in "me and my shadow." For many of us who worked closely with Angeles Arrien, we feel her as a constant companion and advisor as we walk through life. For others, it may be a parent, grandparent, or other role model who is that inseparable companion. This positive shadow companion orients our moral compass and stays by our sides as we do shadow work. Just a few months ago, Angeles appeared to me, on the wall of the Women's Building in San Francisco. Her name emerged from the shadow of the building as I walked past. I had walked by this building at least 50 times without seeing her name. Shadows are like that; they can obscure our vision. Shadows can hide the facts.

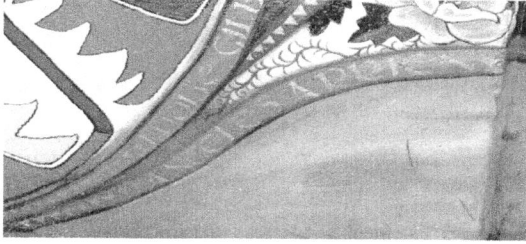

As a verb, the word shadow also has more than one meaning. It can mean *to envelop in darkness,* as in to cast a shadow over something. We are constantly projecting our inner shadow on other people, and they on us. The word shadow can also mean *to follow or observe someone very closely, and usually secretively.* Perhaps our shadow is that secretive spy, watching and manipulating our egos and our thoughts. In our common language, we use the word shadow in varied ways, such as a shadow of a doubt, hiding from one's shadow, to live in someone else's shadow, being afraid of one's own shadow, and the shadow of death. To throw shade means to insult someone, and a shady character has suspect morals and maybe criminal tendencies. Yet on the other hand, we seek out the protection of the cooling shade in summer for relief from the hot sun. Shade takes us out of the glaring spotlight of bright light to a less intense place where we can relax.

Finally, sometimes the origins of words provide some illumination on how the meanings change over time. Shadow seems to have many possible origins from an old Germanic word for darkness and an Old English word that originally meant "to screen or shield from attack," or to protect with covering wings. In the poem *Beowulf,* the evil character Grendel is a called a shadow-goer. In the mid 14th century, a shadow referred to a ghost, and later that century, to foreshadowing, or fortune telling. In the 1690s, the definition of shadow as imitation or copying came into common usage.

Another common use of the term is in the phrase, "shadow-boxing." In its literal use, it means to spar with an invisible partner and is a form of practice. In the psychological literature, it means the process of overcoming a negative self-image that prevents one from achieving success. In both cases, it means to struggle against something you cannot see clearly. Imagine yourself boxing with an invisible opponent—this book will present ways to try to bring that shadowy figure into sharper relief so you can whack those undesirable thoughts back in line with your moral compass. Or to use a less violent image, think of shadow dancing, where we learn to synchronize our movements so that our egos and shadow work together seamlessly, and dance like a synchronized pair of ice dancers.

Fairy tales and myths from across time are stories about the shadow. The evil monsters, giants, ghosts, demons, wicked witches, and evil kings as well as the vindictive gods and goddesses teach us about the struggles between good and evil. The moral of the story helps us address this struggle in our own lives. Marie Louise von-Franz (1997) proposed that the major lesson of fairy tales is that there is always a paradox in challenging life situations, but if we rely on our inner core of being, we can win these battles.

So, shadow has a lot of meanings in our everyday lives, but it becomes an even deeper and more important concept in the hands of psychologists that began to explore it in a systematic way more than a hundred years ago. Philosophers and poets have been aware of it for centuries. Epic battles in the old tales from all lands were journeys to regain one's soul. Shadow is a good metaphor for the qualities that are hidden in the dark recesses of the mind that humans have struggled with throughout time.

3 PSYCHOLOGICAL USES OF SHADOW

"The disowned part of the self is an energy—an emotion or desire or need that has been shamed every time it emerged. These energy patterns are repressed, but not destroyed. They are alive in the unconscious" John Bradshaw

In this chapter and the next, I draw the content mainly from four sources: various works of Angeles Arrien, mostly the *Fourfold Way™* (1993) and my own notes from group sessions and workshops with Angeles where we elaborated on shadow work (Eliason, 2016), writings by Carl Jung (especially *The Undiscovered Self*), Robert Bly's *A Little Book on the Human Shadow* (1988), and David Richo's work, especially *Shadow Dance* (1999). Richo's definition of shadow is perhaps the most clear and understandable, so I will begin with that:

> The shadow is everything about ourselves that we do not know or refuse to know, both dark and light. It is the sum total of the positive and negative traits, feelings, beliefs, and potentials that we refuse to identify as our own. The shadow is that part of us that is incompatible with who we think we are or are supposed to be (1999, p. 1).

Origins of the Shadow

To understand the psychological meanings of the shadow, we need to review some of the terminology used by psychologists to describe the inner workings of our minds and how we interpret and respond to our interior world. Carl Jung recognized the bridge between psychological work and spiritual work that most of the other psychoanalysts of the time ignored. This makes Jung more significant today than ever, when we desperately need more bridging work between science and religion, work on integrating the mind, body, and spirit, and integration work toward wholeness.

Freud's Influence

Some of the terms that are used in shadow work originated from Sigmund Freud, who suggested that our psyche (psyche comes from the

Greek and means self) is made up of three parts: ego, superego, and id. The ego is the part that is most accessible, most in control, and balances out the demands of the id and the ego. The id contains the instinctual and narcissistic drives we are born with to gratify our desires immediately and the superego consists of the learned "rules" of society; the "shoulds" or conscience. The ego also defends us against assaults from the outside world and keeps us functioning. It is vulnerable to influences both from outside of us (needs for approval) and inside of us (unconscious desires that invisibly affect our emotions and behaviors). Freud also suggested that we have three levels of awareness. We have full access to the conscious mind and partial access to the subconscious, the memories, feelings, beliefs, that are just below the surface and pop up often in dreams, slips of the tongue, free associations and intrusive thoughts. We have very limited access to the unconscious, which contains painful things that we repressed through-out our lifetimes and typically cannot access without special techniques like hypnosis. Freud also proposed that we have developed defense mechanisms to protect our egos. These can include denial, repression, rationalizations, and projection. All of these are probably implicated in the development of the shadow. A major area where Jung split from Freud was in regards to Freud's notion that almost all of human behavior was motivated by sexual drives. Another area of contention was Freud's disdain of religion, spirituality, or the popular interest in parapsychological phenomenon that was common in the day. Jung thought that these were worthy of study and had some potential value in understanding the workings of the mind.

Carl Jung's Influence

Jung adopted Freud's notion of the ego and the idea that we do not have full access to all the content of our minds in his work on the shadow but modified these ideas a bit. The Jungians seem to use the idea of the Self as that overarching umbrella term for the inner workings of the mind, which contains the conscious mind, driven by the ego and the unconscious driven by shadow. Sometimes the Self is referred to as the psyche. We have a treasure trove of traits and qualities in the Self, much of which is so buried that we don't have immediate access to it. The ego is the main driver of the conscious aspects of the Self, but is invisibly influenced by the unconscious, that interior world of the good, the bad, and the ugly. David Richo (1999) assures us that the ego is "not a personal fault. It is a conditioned response to the collective setting in which we have always lived" (p. 49) and comes from being in an unawakened state. He thought our egos could be inflated, depleted, or in balance (healthy). The depleted ego, he said "is the opposite of the inflated ego. It is the shadow of the shadow." Pretty deep, huh?

Persona. Then there is the persona. That is the mask that we present to the world—what others see, or at least, what we hope they see. We try to "look good" to the world and hide the things that we don't like about ourselves, or of which others may not approve. Sometimes we are fairly successful in looking good, but often our shadow emerges in our words or behaviors and reveals the stuff we desperately try to hide. The ego is invested in creating, maintaining, and protecting that persona. One of the strategies of the ego is to produce thoughts to protect us. Of course, we need thoughts to survive, but we can get over-identified with our thoughts. On the topic of thoughts, Jung said

> Men are accustomed to seeing thoughts as their very own, so that they eventually confuse them with themselves...your thoughts are just as much outside your self as trees and animals are outside your body (Jung, 2009, p. 186).

When we perceive our thoughts this way, we can recognize that those thoughts are influenced by past events and material in our unconscious mind, and learn to examine them more closely. We tend to think of them as logical and rational, but often they are not; they are products of our ego, influenced by the hidden shadow.

Shadow. Carl Jung wrote extensively about the shadow as it pertained to human motives, thoughts, and behaviors. He believed that everything in the unconscious mind was shadow, and that it affects our behavior profoundly, but largely without our awareness. Jung collapsed Freud's subconscious and unconscious mind into one location or one entity, and proposed that the unconscious contained the content of Freud's id and superego plus much more. He thought that once we repressed something into the shadow, we would have difficulty talking about our feelings—emotions are primitive phenomenon and arise from the shadow, but we cannot always explain why we feel a certain way.

Jung noted "everyone carries a shadow and the less it is embodied in the individual conscious life, the blacker and denser it is." Shadow consists of content such as:

- old primitive instincts that we learned to repress early in our development to obey the "rules" of civilized society;
- the pieces of ourselves we gave away to make others happy, such as gifts, talents, dreams, thoughts, and behaviors that don't meet the expectations of those powerful others (selfishness, need for immediate gratification, artistic talents);
- the traumatic life experiences that we were not ready or willing to face when they happened, so some part of our minds pushed them down to the unconscious realm;
- memories, thoughts, and feelings that we have forgotten over time. We needed to repress some of our instincts and behaviors in order to live a civilized life with others, but some of what we repressed or forgot are qualities, traits, or memories that could serve us well today. We just ran out of space in our conscious mind to hold these memories;
- Shadow also contains intuition. This is wisdom that shows up suddenly, without any explanation for how or where the idea came from. We just know it to be true.

Jung thought that a fear of abandonment develops in most of us, because we learned to give up parts of ourselves to prevent losing a parent's love and approval. We gave up some of our instinctual behaviors, like need for instant gratification, or we gave up life dreams for fear of losing the approval or love of others, so later any hint of that shadow may re-trigger the abandonment fears. Society also forces us to repress characteristics like selfishness and greed so that the greater good can be served. We go along with this to earn the approval of others, but they are also necessary for civilized society. Angeles Arrien suggested that the two major fears related to our relationships are fear of abandonment and fear of entrapment—we can have both fears simultaneously or have mainly one or the other fear. When we have both, we may exhibit a "push-pull" dynamic in our relationships, clinging to others at times and pushing them away when we fear being trapped or pinned down. Both types of fears co-exist in the shadow.

The shadow is a junk heap of many layers, according to Jung, with most of the top layers coming from our unique personal experiences, which he called the personal unconscious. The bottom layer comes from neglected or repressed aspects of our broader communities and ancestors. He labeled this the "collective unconscious," and it comes from our evolution as human beings. Archetypes and instincts are in the collective unconscious. We carry shadow that is both personal and unique to us, and shadow that is shared by others like us, in "the long bag we drag behind us" (Robert Bly, 1988). But this bag full of shadows is not passive; over time it "devolves toward barbarism" and causes harm (Bly, 1988). Bly also stated "every part of our personality that we do not love will become hostile to us." We need to get it out in the light so we can deal with it. Zwieg and Wolf (1997) noted that the personal shadow contains the stuff that our parents, families, or cultures deemed as forbidden, taboo, or shameful. These can be different things to different families/cultures. One set of parents may denigrate intellectual pursuits while another devalues artistic endeavors. A culture may value competition and individual effort over cooperation and the collective. All the experts agree that if we do not deal with our shadow, it will wreak havoc in our lives. Jung, writing about a person who had not acknowledged his shadow, said, "there is, after all, no harsher bitterness than that of a person who is his own worst enemy" (1961, p. 152).

The Shadow Over a Lifetime

Carl Jung's autobiography (1961) begins, "my life is a story of the self-realization of the unconscious" (p. 1). He began to struggle with shadow even in childhood, and his life is marked by significant visions and dreams that led him to discover the inner workings of the mind. Most of us did not start this awareness of the unconscious mind or shadow until much later in life. Robert Bly suggested "we spend our lives until we're twenty deciding what parts of ourselves to put in the bag [shadow], and we spend the rest of our lives trying to get them out again." Perceived or actual rejection by parents and society happens before we can even talk, so often we carry this pain of rejection in a pre-verbal place, making it harder to name or identify. David Richo and Angeles Arrien also commented on the lifespan development of shadow. In the first half of life, we are building up and inflating our egos in search of power and status—thus many of our good qualities are shoved into the shadow if they don't support our need for power and material things. We develop "blind spots" where we cannot see the things that might be apparent to others around us. Richo described the negative aspects of shadow as being in the cellar and the positive aspects as being relegated to the attic. While working on this book, I had a dream about climbing up the ladder to the attic of my childhood home. Once there, I found all sorts of trinkets that I dispersed as gifts to the people downstairs. The attic was not dark and scary, but a place of treasures that gave me much pleasure to share with others.

Angeles said that the first half of life is about doing and acquiring, which are often associated with giving up parts of our selves so that we can get the needed approval of others that ensures our success. We have to make compromises to fit into the world of work, family, community, and intimate relationships. The second half of life is about seeking meaning and integration, which necessitates integrating our shadow back into our sense of self and reclaiming what we gave up earlier.

Dreams

Carl Jung wrote a lot about the manifestations of the shadow in dreams, but cautioned against dream analysis in therapy or by using guides to dream analysis that assumed that symbols and archetypes in dreams had universal meanings. He noted

> No dream symbol can be separated from the individual who dreams it and there is no definite or straightforward interpretation of any dream. Each individual varies so much in the way that his unconscious complements or compensates his conscious mind that it is impossible to be sure how far dreams and their symbols can be classified at all (Jung, 1964, p. 38).

It took Jung years to understand his own dreams, much less the dreams of other people. He suggested that even common motifs in dreams such as flying, falling, being chased, and being unclothed in public, have no meaning alone—they must be considered in the whole context of the dream. The unconscious communicates in a different way than our conscious minds which use language and logic. Shadow communications are via images, symbols, and archetypes that are filtered through our own life experiences and exposures. We might interpret them through our religious upbringing, our own knowledge of and study of mythology, or we may interpret them in our own unique way. Joseph Campbell said that dreams can emerge from the unconscious as "little dreams" from the personal unconscious and as "big dreams" from the collective unconscious. These big dreams are full of myth, symbols, and are in "technicolor."

Projection

One of the psychological defense mechanisms of the ego originally proposed by Sigmund Freud is a process called projection. This is when we defend ourselves against or disown an unconscious impulse by denying its existence while at the same time, attributing it to another person. Jung thought that one of the most common ways that shadow manifests is through projection. In projection, we take one of our own shadow qualities and cast it onto another person. Angeles said that we can recognize projections because they carry an "energetic charge." For example, I may strongly dislike a co-worker who never really did anything negative to me, but who I believe has "control issues." I may have this strong reaction because I myself have unacknowledged control issues. But I don't just casually note, "oh, she has control issues." Instead, I have a lot of feeling behind it, "I really dislike the way that she tries to control the situation," I say with a bit of venom in my voice. Sometimes we strongly dislike someone almost the minute we meet them; there must be some shadow projection going on, as we do not have enough information upon which to base an opinion. As Robert Bly put it, "our psyche in daily life tries to give us a hint of where our shadow lies by picking out people to hate in an irrational way." That experience of hatred, which certainly carries an energetic charge, is the shadow waving a red flag. Here I am, pay attention to me, it says.

If we do not recognize the presence of shadow in these projections, Jung said that we draw a "thickening veil of illusion" between our egos and the real world. But on the other hand, Jung also said, "in spite of its function as a reservoir for human darkness—or perhaps because of this—the shadow is the seat of creativity." The dark and the light always co-exist and feed off of each other. Marie Louise von Franz, a student of Jung, also added that if we did not project, we might never connect with the world, but noted that we cannot just project in the abstract. If we do not have personal contact with the people on which we project, we can do harm to them and to ourselves, because we do not see them as they really are. This might explain why some people can get so fixated and obsessed with celebrities. Without any actual contact with the person, our projections can remain intact (and distort our ability to see them as real flawed human beings).

Katie and Gay Hendricks (2018) suggested that there are three ways we can know when we are projecting. These reactions indicate that some old trauma or narcissistic tendency from our past has been triggered:

1. We feel righteous—we are absolutely certain that we are right and the other is wrong.

2. We feel that we have been wronged. We feel a sense of sadness or hurt, even if the situation is rather minor.

3. The situation feels like "life or death." A sense of panic or anxiety arises.

If someone else is projecting onto me, well, I may not be aware of it. But if I do suspect that it is happening, my response should be to "stay in my own lane." The projection is the other person's making and not related to anything I have done. If this is someone close to me, I might be able to talk to them about it and find out their perspective and share my thoughts. However, I cannot do the shadow work for the other person, and I have enough work on my hands to address my own shadow. What I can do, is treat the person with compassion and eventually the projection will "wobble" and be more likely to be dispelled. Jungian analyst Robert Johnson (1991) said that it is possible to refuse a projection from another person, but only after we have done a lot of shadow work ourselves. Otherwise, when someone projects on us, our own shadow is activated and we become reactive and defensive. The best bet, according to Johnson, is to stay grounded and not take the bait.

Individuation

We get glimpses of our shadow traits in these projections onto others, but also in dreams, visions, and in times of individuation or maturation phases. Jung said that when we have a strong sense of restlessness, loss of meaning, and boredom with our present lives, we are entering a period of individuation (a process of seeking wholeness). Angeles Arrien called these feelings a "divine discontent" that signaled a need to do soul retrieval work. Soul retrieval was her term for illuminating and integrating the shadow. Whether we call it individuation or soul retrieval, these are periods of intense personal growth. This individuation process, as both Jung and Angeles described it, involves a descent into the unconscious to identify these shadow aspects, and following up with work to make peace with the shadow. Once we have befriended some aspect of shadow, we experience an ascent to greater self-awareness. First we have to descend inside of ourselves to work on the shadow issue. The goal is to become aware of and accept the shadow, but not identify or attach to it. If we attach to it, the shadow side may dominate our behavior for a while. We go to the "dark side of the force"—it turns out that Darth Vader is everyone's father! Eventually, we emerge on the other side, integrate the knowledge of the shadow into our psyche, and ascend as a better, more self-aware person. About that danger of identifying with the shadow, Jung said, "A man who is possessed by his shadow is always standing in his own light and falling into his own traps...living below his own level." So we need to identify and befriend the shadow without attaching to it. When we project the shadow onto others, we give away our power and feel the loss of energy—reclaiming our shadow restores our inner power source of vitality.

Befriending the Shadow

Robert Bly developed a model using projection that he called "eating the shadow" which will be described in more detail in the last section of practices. In short, this is a method of incorporating shadow aspects of the self that have been projected onto others back into our conscious psyche. Bly thought that there were actions we could take to foster this process along, such as writing about it in the form of journaling or poetry (Bly considered certain types of language including poetry as "nets" to capture the shadow), drumming, solitude, and other contemplative practices. He suggested that when we feel hatred toward another person, we should break eye contact (to avoid harm to them), disrupt the hatred, and look to the right. He thought that the shadow would then emerge and we could honor it. First, honor it by naming it (I feel anger or envy or an urge for revenge in this situation) and then we talk to it as if it were a person (What do you want from me?). These processes honor the feelings/shadows without having to express them or repress them. Of course, this is predicated on the idea that we recognize a shadow projection for what it is. For a fascinating account of how Jung engaged with his own shadow and his dialogue with the archetypes that arose in his dreams and visions, see *The Red Book* published in 2009, long after his death.

Angeles added to this discussion about befriending the shadow in the *Second Half of Life,* when she proposed that a major task of maturation is the ability to dispense with dualities. Historians noted that most of the ancient religions of the world recognized that we needed the dark side of the personality and had rituals and methods of bringing together our egos and shadow in a slow steady fashion. But with the rise of Christianity, the dualities were polarized into God/Satan, Good/Evil, Heaven/Hell, and Light/Dark. Christianity sought to abolish or at least suppress the darker forces, resulting in the split psyche we have today that resists addressing the shadow. Joseph Campbell described these dualities as two horns—if we get hooked on either horn, we die. He proposed that there are always more than just two sides, and that we can hold the opposites at the same time. When we do that, the other options emerge.

I'll never forgot the first time I heard someone ask Angeles a question about what they should, framing it as an either/or question. The person said something to the effect as "Should I honor my commitment to staying with my spouse through sickness and in health or leave my marriage?" Angeles responded "yes." At first I thought this was just a joke. It took some careful reflection on the matter to realize that she truly believed in "both/and" solutions to problems. This answer also emphasized to the one asking the question that they had to find the answer within themselves, rather than seek outside guidance.

To be mature adults, we need to give up either/or thinking and embrace the both/and. For example, I do not have to consider myself as a judgmental person or not judgmental. I am both/and: judgmental sometimes, but more often not. Embracing paradox is a sign of developing wisdom. I learn to name the shadow, stay aware of it, but not indulge it. Bly stressed that shadow work is "shady dealing" and not to be done in public, or we may harm others. Shadow energies are only destructive when ignored or expressed to others through unconscious projections.

Richo's Work on Ego

David Richo (1999) focused a lot of his shadow work on developing a healthy ego, which requires addressing the shadow. His definition of Self as "the psychic totality which contains ego consciousness and transcends it" (p. 78) considers the unclaimed shadow qualities as "pure unbounded potentiality" (p. 78). Richo thought that if we let go of aspects of the unhealthy ego (fear, attachment, control, entitlement), the Self would emerge and bring a healthy quality to take the place of what we let go. He noted that psychological work on the ego opens us up to spiritual work on the Self. Positive aspects of ourselves that we have not yet claimed is the "truth in waiting" in the Self (p. 98). For example, he noted that when we let go of the urge to punish (psychological work on the ego), we can instead seek to rehabilitate or heal (spiritual work). When we let go of the need to fight, this frees up the ability to negotiate. When we let go of grudges, we can forgive. Several of Richo's ego exercises are listed in the practices section to encourage letting go of unhealthy ego behaviors. When the shadow is in the driver's seat, the ego is unhealthy.

4 ANGELES ARRIEN AND SHADOW

"The major shadow aspect of the Visionary archetype is self-abandonment. Human beings universally abandon themselves for five major reasons: for someone's love; for someone's acceptance and approval; to keep the peace; to maintain balance; or to stay in a state of harmony" (Arrien, 1993, p. 94).

In reviewing Angeles' books and going over my notes from sessions with her over a long period of time, it seems that much of Angeles' work was focused on getting at shadow characteristics and integrating them into the self. She talked a lot about "soul retrieval" or the reclaiming of the bits and pieces we gave up of ourselves to be successful in the world or to get the approval of some powerful others—all those pieces are there, in the shadow. Angeles' program was all about learning to live a more authentic life. This cannot be accomplished without shadow work. Three different areas of Angeles' work seemed the most ripe for individual or small group shadow work. In this section, I talk about 1) the shadow side of the four archetypes, 2) projection/mirror work, and 3) the notion of the primary and secondary process. Each of these concepts lend themselves to self-reflective approaches to identifying shadow. Exercises based on these ideas can be found in the practices section.

The Shadow Aspects of the Four Archetypes

The idea of archetypes as part of our unconscious mind comes mostly from Carl Jung's work, who said that part of the collective unconscious are the mythic patterns of behaviors or instincts that have served the world for generations. We needed them to survive at some point in time. We inherit these archetypes and always have access to them because they are a part of the evolution of our brains. I found different definitions of archetypes: sometimes they were described as mythic figures, like gods, goddesses, angels, or demons. Sometimes they were defined as life roles, like the hero, the innocent, the rebel, the explorer, the sage, the magician. Yet other times, they were presented as situations, such life, death, and rebirth scenarios, life turning points, and so on. David Richo noted, "archetypes are psychic dispositions or instincts that enable us to activate the spiritual possibilities of the Self."

He thought that the ego could be threatened by archetypes. Who wants to face their inner Medusa, after all? But if we allow them to come into conscious awareness, the ego can incorporate and integrate archetypes into our repertoire of human behaviors. Archetypes tend to come in pairs of opposites: heroes and villains, good and evil, human and divine, wise person and trickster.

One story that Angeles often told came from North American indigenous peoples, and was the idea that we all have two wolves inside of us, one pure evil and the other good. When an elder is asked which one will win, the answer is "the one we feed." To feed the good, we have to be aware of the evil and keep it within sight. The evil wolf is still inside of us, but we keep it in control by not feeding it any fuel.

Angeles used the idea of archetypes and their shadow characteristics in a unique way in her *FourFold Way™* approach. Jung places archetypes, or universal models or prototypes for human qualities or types into the collective unconscious shadow, so archetypes are largely unconscious influences in his model. On the other hand, Angeles focused on four universal archetypes that she found in her study of indigenous cultures around the world: the warrior or leader, healer, teacher, and visionary (a truth-teller). We can readily recognize whether we have these archetypes once we study them, although they may have been buried in our psyches for a long time before we begin the process of learning about them and cultivating them in our lives.

In Angeles' model, each archetype has both positive characteristics and shadow aspects. If a person is very strong in one archetype, they may have a tendency to over-identify with it, and run the risk of showing the shadow side of the archetype. George R.R. Martin said, "The brightest flame casts the deepest shadow." Yes, I did it; I put a Game of Thrones reference here. After all, it is an epic tale of archetypes and family and cultural shadow! Game of Thrones is a modern day fairy tale with complicated people who are both good and evil, and who struggle with their shadow. I think the popularity of this show is a testimony for the need to break down dualistic thinking like simple good or evil and to witness people actually wrestling with their shadow.

People who do their work to strengthen, open, deepen, and soften all the archetypes, are relatively balanced and tend to have less shadow. The chart below shows the positive and shadow aspects of each archetype (see Arrien, 1993 for more detail).

Archetype	Positive Characteristics	Shadow Aspects
Warrior	Leadership skills, right use of power, knows what we stand for and by. Sets limits and boundaries, respects self and others. Embodies courage and presence. Principle: Show up and be present	Rebelling against authority, hiding or holding back from showing our best selves, preferring to work behind the scenes rather than step up, latching onto more powerful people and riding their coattails.
Healer	Uses the healing power of love to care for inner self and outer world. Cultivation of compassion. Principle: Pay attention to what has heart and meaning.	Addictions to perfectionism, intensity, needing to know, or focusing on what is not working instead of what works. Not engaging in self-care.
Visionary	Sees the big picture, lives in truth and authenticity. Vision brings our creative fire into the world. Principle: Tell the truth without blame or judgment.	Editing, hiding, rehearsing one's speech rather than speaking truth, loss of sense of humor, giving up parts of self for approval or to keep the peace, getting over-identified or fixed on one point of view.
Teacher	Wisdom stems from trust and is flexible and fluid. Cares deeply from a place of non-attachment. Principle: Be open, not attached to outcomes.	Stubbornly stick to one opinion, judging others, saying things at the wrong time or place, trying to be in control, feeling confused about the right action to take.

In the practices section, you will find an assessment tool to measure your shadow characteristics for each of the four archetypes. This activity will help you consider if you might be over-identified in one or more areas. For now, use the positive qualities to consider which archetypes are strongest in you at this time, and which ones need to be strengthened. Which of the principles comes easiest to you and which is the hardest?

Projection/Mirror Work

Angeles did not often use the psychological language of projection, because she was a cultural anthropologist who specialized in cross-cultural signs and symbols. But she clearly found evidence of the shadow in all the indigenous peoples that she studied, and she used the symbol of the mirror to study projections. She said "if I see it in another person, I have it in myself." That is, we see things in others that made us feel comfortable to be ourselves, that bring out the best in us, that signal feelings of envy or dislike or attraction, or sometimes, that person barely even registers with us. Angeles noted "the motif of the mirror, as a metaphor of reflection, is found cross-culturally...those who are mirrors for us become our teachers and demonstrate ways that we may reclaim authenticity" (1993, p. 95).

The types of mirrors that she worked with include:

- **Clear mirror**: this person teaches us about our best self. If I see positive qualities in another person, I have them in me as well. I can own it. A clear mirror is a person who captures our imagination and who carries a lot of positive energy for us—someone who ignites the fires of inspiration. So these projections give us a clue to the positive characteristics that we have, but have suppressed or not acknowledged.
- **Neutral mirror**: this is a person I'm so comfortable with that I can just be myself. I need no effort or performance and feel calm and at home with this person. There may not be any projection going on here, or we may be projecting our own persona onto these people to create a sense of sameness (and safety).
- **Smoking mirror**: This person shows where my negative shadow work is; I'm projecting my own negative stuff on another person. The person who irritates and annoys me can be my best teacher related to shadow work. This person may spark competition, jealousy, or envy (comparison). They bring up "unfinished business" or remind us of someone from our past. Most importantly, they display a quality that we do not want to acknowledge in ourselves.

- **Split mirror:** There are two types. In the fire type of split mirror, this is a person to whom I am sexually attracted. It's important to acknowledge these feelings to avoid feeding off the sexual energy and sending a mixed message. David Richo and others have written a lot about how sexual attraction really triggers projections. When we meet someone we are attracted to, we project all the positive qualities we want in a partner onto them. We don't see them as they are, but as we want them to be. Sometimes we are sorely disappointed when we start to see them as real human beings. In the second form of split mirror, the power-type, this is the person to whom we give away our power. It's someone with whom we may have approval needs, or don't totally trust. We might feel intimidated by this person. Both types of split mirrors may be projections.
- **No mirror:** This is the person who is present, but that I have not seen or interacted with. It is important to discern why this person has not registered with me—why have I overlooked this unique individual? This person may represent a part of myself that I have subconsciously rendered invisible or do not want others to see. Who in your workplace, extended family, personal growth group, or other circumstances do you have trouble seeing? Who is the person who is "there" but you never talk to? Is there someone in your workplace or social network whose name you cannot remember?

You will find an activity in the practices section where you can explore who in your life serves these mirror functions and consider what this has to say about your shadow. You will also find a practice for turning the mirror inward to start seeing ourselves more realistically.

Primary and Secondary Process

Angeles taught that whenever another person is speaking, there are two processes going on simultaneously in the listeners. The primary process is the topic itself, and the facts about the situation the person is describing. The secondary process is related to the listener's own feelings about the speaker, judgements about what they say, old memories that are triggered by the person's words or body language, impatience that leads to jumping to a conclusion before listening to the end, and many other inner responses. If the speaker is telling a story about traumatic events, this may trigger painful memories and defense mechanisms to block those memories from overwhelming the listener. It seems to me that this is all shadow stuff. Let me give an example of how this works.

Once when it was my turn to facilitate a FourFold Way study group, I decided to explore these two processes more directly. There were six or seven people present that evening, and we started with one person sharing a current dilemma—a situation where she needed to take some action and wanted some guidance from the group. She shared without interruption for about five minutes, and then I asked the group to take three minutes to write what they thought the heart of the matter was—what was the problem that needed solving? What questions did they want to ask the speaker to clarify the issue? This would be the primary process. When that three minutes was up, I asked them to write about their secondary process. What did this situation bring up for them in terms of old memories, being in a similar situation in the past, feelings or reactions to the sharing of the story, feelings about the person doing the sharing, and so on. I told them that they should be as honest as possible and would not be asked to share this part of the exercise unless they felt comfortable doing so. I thought it would be safer to talk about the processes and general learning that came up, rather than the content of the writing.

My expectation was that everyone would have a similar assessment of the heart of the matter that the person shared. Much to my surprise, when we went around the circle and shared what the topic and the dilemma to be addressed was, there was a wide range of responses. Some thought that the heart of the matter was a conflict between loyalties to one's partner versus biological family, another thought the issue was time management, another thought it was an issue of the person doing the sharing neglecting their own self-care, and so on. We did not agree on the basic "facts" of the issue. WTF??

Upon reflection, I think that the secondary process got activated so quickly that everyone listened and responded from their own shadow perspective, not the position of the speaker or the "facts." The shadow is activated so soon in a conversation that we respond from that unconscious place, not from a detached, objective, deep listening perspective. The situation that the person shared was one that did not carry a great deal of emotional charge to it, and I suspect that more emotional or raw sharing would have elicited even greater activation of shadow. If you have a group that does personal work, you might want to try out this activity and see what it brings forth. We had a very rich discussion that night.

Have you ever had this experience where the "facts" seemed crystal clear to you, but other people had a vastly different interpretation?

***

What consequences did this lack of a shared understanding of the problem have in this group?

***

How did you resolve the difference?

.

5 PRACTICES

*"You already own the costly elixir that will heal.
You have only to use it" Rumi*

Much to my chagrin, I have learned that I cannot do shadow work by merely reading books or thinking about it. I've spent most of my life convinced that I could learn everything I needed to know from books and my own powers of rational thinking, but it only takes me so far. If we only contemplate our life experiences, we never get beyond the knowledge of our egos. Reflection work is necessary, but not enough— we also need to integrate our shadow. This requires stepping into the unknown. Yikes, give me a nice safe book any day!

The reading I have done on the shadow suggests that it emerges often and we might be able to catch glimpses of it through a variety of activities. Most of us do not want to wait until a shadow aspect reveals itself in a dream or vision. We may desire to take some conscious actions or engage in some regular contemplative practices to push them into the light so that we can deal with them. Of course, dream journals may be helpful, but there are other ways to identify shadow that are more under our direct control and don't take years to interpret. To make any sustainable change in our lives, we need a daily practice. Angeles Arrien (2005, p. 28) said

> Practice is meant to be active, rigorous, and dynamic...to practice is to take daily action that supports change...both reflection and practice are essential to cultivating wisdom.

So at the end of each practice, spend a little time considering what daily action you can take to support a change in this area. Those shadow qualities won't just integrate themselves. We might need to do some work to strengthen our warrior to give us the courage to face our demons, or our healer to help us with self-compassion. Shadow work requires a little help and encouragement from our conscious and deliberate actions.

This section contains the meat of shadow work (or for the vegetarian readers, the tofu). I give several examples of reflective exercises that help to identify shadow aspects of the self, ending with two practices aimed at integrating the shadow: methods proposed by David Richo and Robert Bly for reintegrating those aspects into our conscious minds. These different methods may be effective at highlighting different aspects of the shadow, or may show different shadow qualities at different times, depending on what is current in your life at the moment. There are many examples here, and hopefully one or some of them will resonate with you personally. Since we are all unique individuals, there are no "one size fits all" ways to address our shadow. On the other hand, if you resist any of the activities in the next section, that might be a sign that a shadow is activated. We are often driven by fear when faced with dealing with the unconscious. The shadow is so full of stuff that we have denied and repressed, that when we have to face the shadows, it's natural that our egos resist looking them in the face. Note when you feel resistance or shame, and pay attention to what seems to lie beneath it. That's where the real work lies—the deeper we go, the more likely we are getting to shadow. If you cannot face it head on yet, look sideways and get a glimpse until it's not so scary.

Contemplating the Shadow Indirectly

Famous writers have had a lot to say about the shadow, some of which is compatible with the teachings of Carl Jung, Robert Bly, and Angeles Arrien. Robert Bly noted that some types of writing are "nets" to capture the shadow. I have listed a few examples on the following pages. For each one, think about whether this statement rings true for you, and whether you can relate it to a specific event or period in your life. If so inclined, journal about what the quotation means to you and notice if any hint of shadow qualities emerges from the contemplation. Journaling is the oldest tool for self-reflection, as Angeles noted, and often insights can emerge from structured or unstructured journaling. In addition, analysts like Freud and Jung used various forms of free association to get at the shadow.

To try out a version of free associating, set a timer for five minutes. Then read one prompt, start writing, and then just keep going with whatever thoughts come to you, whether they seem related to the quote or not. Don't stop until the timer goes off. In many cases, a symbol, an old memory, a forgotten or repressed idea might emerge from what seems to be a meaningless rambling. Jung complained that his search for his inner world was a struggle between sense and nonsense (Jung, 1961). The nonsense comes from the unconscious, but it eventually starts to make sense if we pay close attention.

Free Associating to Quotes

D.H. Lawrence: "Are you willing to be sponged out, erased, canceled, made nothing? If not, you will never really change."

***

Walt Whitman: "Keep your face always toward the sunshine and the shadows will fall behind you."

***

Friedrich Nietzsche "Thoughts are the shadows of our feelings—always darker, emptier, and simpler."

***

Angeles Arrien: "Every day we choose anew whether we will support the authentic self or the false self."

***

Paulo Coelho: "Love is a trap, when it appears, we see only its light, not its shadows."

***

Carl Jung: "What we resist, persists."

***

Elie Wiesel: "Most people think that shadows follow, precede, or surround beings or objects. The truth is that they also surround words, ideas, desires, impulses, and memories."

***

Thomas Browne: "Life itself is but the shadow of death and souls departed but the shadows of the living."

***

Blaise Pascal: "In faith, there is enough light for those who want to believe and enough shadows to blind those who don't."

***

Theodore Dreiser: "Words are but the vague shadows of the volumes we mean. Little audible links, they are, chaining together great inaudible feelings and purposes."

***

Jacob Norby: "Every pain, anguish, addiction, longing, depression, anger or fear is an orphaned part of us seeking joy; some disowned shadow wanting to return to the light and home of ourselves."

***

Gilles Deleuze "The shadow escapes from the body like an animal we had been sheltering."

***

Parker Palmer: "There are no shortcuts to wholeness. The only way to become whole is to put our arms lovingly around everything we've shown ourselves to be: self-serving and generous, spiteful and compassionate, cowardly and courageous, treacherous and trustworthy. We must be able to say to ourselves and to the world at large, I am all of the above."

***

Rumi: The Guest House

This being human is a guest house.
Every morning a new arrival.
A joy, a depression, a meanness,
some momentary awareness comes
as an unexpected visitor.
Welcome and entertain them all!
Even if they are a crowd of sorrows,
who violently sweep your house
empty of its furniture,
still, treat each guest honorably.
He may be clearing you out
for some new delight.
The dark thought, the shame, the malice.
meet them at the door laughing and invite them in.
Be grateful for whatever comes.
because each has been sent
as a guide from beyond.

Self-Abandonment

Angeles Arrien (1993) noted that we abandon pieces of our true selves and lose our sense of integrity for five basic reasons. These are:

1. To gain someone's love
2. To get someone's approval
3. To keep the peace
4. To maintain balance in a relationship
5. To stay in a state of harmony.

For this practice, we will consider situations in childhood and then in adulthood when we abandoned our values, our boundaries, our creative interests, our life dreams, or took a different path in life than we wanted, all to satisfy the demands of another person.

Thinking of your childhood, what pieces of yourself did you abandon, and for which reason? Describe at least one situation in some detail and consider what could be reclaimed now to promote healing.

***

Thinking of your adult relationships, have you noticed any patterns in self-abandonment? That is, do you appease and give in to others for the same reason over and over? Do you have a pattern?

***

Write about a recent or particularly challenging relationship issue when you abandoned a piece of yourself, and discuss how you can go about reclaiming that lost piece.

Introducing Paradox

One skill that we need to acquire to be successful at shadow work is the ability to recognize and hold life's paradoxes. Jung mentioned this often. In his book on Dream Analysis (1929), he said:

> It is a bewildering thing in human life that the thing that is the greatest fear is the source of the greatest wisdom. One's greatest foolishness is one's biggest stepping stone. No one can be a wise man without being a terrible fool. Through Eros one learns the truth, through sins we learn virtue.

So if we can reframe the way we look at our mistakes, regrets, embarrassments, and other human foibles, we are on a path to wisdom. The following questions were inspired by the quote from Jung.

What is your greatest fear? Name it and hold it in your mind as long as you can. What is the wisdom that might lie behind looking at that fear?

***

Think of a time when you felt foolish. What did it lead to when you got over the embarrassment? If you still feel shame, what could lie beyond the shame?

***

When in your life has acting like a fool led to some kernel of wisdom? How did you transform the foolish moments to the gold of wisdom? What was your alchemical formula?

***

What is an action or thought that you labelled as sinful or unacceptable in yourself? What is the virtue on the other side of that act/thought?

The Shadow of the Ego

David Richo (1999) explored the concept of the healthy versus unhealthy ego. The healthy ego conducts itself in mature, direct ways, while the unhealthy ego comes from the shadow and is often immature, indirect, and passive-aggressive. The unhealthy ego is not connected to the inner wisdom voice or intuition. If we use the metaphor of the ego as the driver of our self, the unhealthy ego is an impaired driver. The shadow drinks, drives, texts, and eats nachos while driving, and it causes accidents. It is a gas guzzler, using up all of our energy and resources, and does not produce the results we want. We get to the wrong destination or drive around in circles for hours. But, as Richo noted, when we let go of a shadow of the ego, the healthy side emerges automatically. The table below shows the two sides of the coin that is the ego.

The healthy ego:	The unhealthy ego (driven by shadow):
Observes	Denies, dissects
Assesses objectively, in a detached manner	Judges, blames
Acts with information from the assessing	Does not use information, but follows emotions or old patterns
Learns from mistakes	Repeats mistakes
Is present	Lives in the past or future
Is not moved by fear	Caught up in fears and clings to old ways
Aligns behavior with values/meaning	Appeases or gives into demands from others
Makes and keeps commitments	Is driven by fear of abandonment or entrapment and breaks commitments
Considers decisions in detached manner	Is impulsive or obsessive
Takes responsibility	Feels victimized by others or circumstances
Is self-driven	Driven by outside forces
Engages in creative problem-solving	Falls back on old habits or patterns of behavior

Has a serene, positive energy	Has a nervous or anxious energy

In the first activity about ego shadows, think of a recent difficult situation in which you found yourself and felt that you did not handle as well as you wished. Did one of these shadows of ego drive your thoughts, words, or behaviors? What was it and how did it affect the outcome of the situation?

***

What would you have said or done differently if the healthy ego had been in charge?

***

Next, consider the table above of shadows of the ego, and circle or underline the ones that are common problems for you. Then prioritize the list—which one(s) will you work on first, and how can you start to recognize when it is in the driver's seat? That is, what seems to activate the unhealthy ego quality?

***

Later, we will complicate this idea that the ego is healthy or unhealthy. When we start to break down the dualisms and consider both/and possibilities, we will start to find more balance. When we befriend the shadow, we become more aware when we are engaging in unhealthy ego practices, and can change course.

What's in Your Family Shadow?

"Maybe this is the one who will break the destructive family patterns..."
Angeles Arrien

One corner of the shadow contains material that comes from our upbringing in families. According to Connie Zweig and Steve Wolf (1997), every family has a "soul" that has been sacrificed to maintain the family persona. In the U.S., a common family persona is the Judeo-Christian image of the honest, hard-working, God-loving, church-goer. But depending on ethnicity, religious upbringing, socioeconomic status, educational levels, and other factors, that family persona may differ. Some may favor an artsy, bohemian persona, or a "professional" family or others. Anything in the child that distorts the family persona will get punished or pushed to the shadow. You might be able to identify those shadow characteristics through the following questions:

What was/is your family of origin persona? What image did your parents try to present to the outside world?

***

What behaviors were you punished for?

***

How did your parents express emotions? How did they encourage or discourage you from expressing how you felt?

***

What things did you do that your family caused you to feel shame or guilt about?

Zweig and Wolf (1997) noted that "the elders' hidden conflicts, anxious worries, and buried wishes are absorbed by vulnerable young minds...like little sponges, children pick up hatreds, depressions, fears, and addictions, even if they have never been mentioned aloud" (p. 64).

What were the unspoken shadow qualities of the family elders that you absorbed?

***

What were the family secrets?

Family Triangles

In some families, one family member is made the scapegoat to reduce the conflict between other family members, usually parents. For example, instead of lashing out at his wife, a father may choose one child who has similar behaviors to the mother to take out his anger and frustration. This may set siblings against each other as well. Another common scenario is when a parent is envious of a child or sees them as a rival for the partner's attention and love.

Do/Did you have a family triangle?

***

Did one parent belittle the other in front of the children, setting off a dynamic of children taking the side of the belittler to avoid being verbally abused as well?

***

Was any child in the family seen as a rival for the attention of a parent?

***

What effect has this had on your adult life?

Common Shadows in Families

We learn so many things from our families, and many of these carry shadows of envy, greed, guilt, shame, anger, anxiety—all of which can lead to substance abuse, depression, suicide behaviors. Zweig and Wolf (1997) noted that "shame is a gatekeeper of family shadow." Explore some of the possible shame-laden shadow aspects that are found in many families.

What did you learn from your family about

- money
- what gives a person self worth
- how you should feel about your body and sexuality
- how people are supposed to communicate with each other
- what religious beliefs you should have

In the quote that begins this section, Angeles Arrien was referring to an indigenous saying about the ancestors, expressing the wish that someone in the current generation would break the old patterns and lead the family into new and more healthy ways. Are you that one? Angeles would ask.

What would it take to break unhealthy patterns in your current immediate family or your family of origin?

***

What skills do you have to become "the one?"

Identifying the Shadow Side of the Four Archetypes

This exercise uses the shadow aspects of the four archetypes that Angeles Arrien worked with in the *Fourfold Way™*. The following assessment tool draws from the shadow aspects of each archetype that are named in the *Fourfold Way™* book (Arrien, 1993). This may show you where you are over-identified with one or more archetypes. If you are out of balance, this indicates the need to strengthen the other archetypes to get back in balance. Recognizing where you are over-identified helps you to re-balance within an archetype. For example, if you find yourself often responding to authority with rebellion, consider who is harmed by this rebellion, and what might underlie it. Is it a need to be control? A fear of abandonment? A need to be "different?" If you are a healer, particularly as your career or vocation, you may be at risk for ignoring your own self care because you focus your attention on others. Ultimately, you cannot be an effective healer of others unless you take good care of yourself first.

In this table, W=Warrior; H=Healer; V=Visionary; and T=Teacher. Refer to the FourFold Way book (Arrien, 1993) for ideas of how to develop or strengthen each archetype.

How true of you are these statements at this time in your life?	Never/ Rarely	Sometimes	Often	Almost Always
W1. I rebel against authority just for the sake of rebellion.	0	1	2	3
W2. I have issues with authority figures even when there is no specific reason for it.	0	1	2	3
W3. I hide or hold back my best work.	0	1	2	3
W4. I prefer to work behind the scenes rather than be recognized for my contribution.	0	1	2	3
W5. I tend to latch onto more powerful people and ride their coattails.	0	1	2	3
H1. I get caught up in drama, feeding on the energy of it.	0	1	2	3
H2. I cannot bring a task to completion until it is "perfect."	0	1	2	3
H3. I have a great need to know everything that is going on.	0	1	2	3
H4. I tend to focus on what is not working rather than what it working.	0	1	2	3
H5. I do not take care of myself as well as I care for others.	0	1	2	3
V1. I edit my thoughts and speech rather than speak my truth.	0	1	2	3
V2. I hide my true opinion.	0	1	2	3
V3. I have lost my sense of humor.	0	1	2	3
V4. I give up parts of myself to get acceptance, approval, or keep the peace.	0	1	2	3
V5. I get over-identified with my own point of view.	0	1	2	3

T1. I stubbornly stick to one position rather than be open to alternatives.	0	1	2	3
T2. I find myself judging others.	0	1	2	3
T3. I sometimes say things at the wrong time or place.	0	1	2	3
T4. I try to get control over situations.	0	1	2	3
T5. I often feel confused about the right action to take.	0	1	2	3

Add up the scores for each section separately:

W1-5 (Warrior) = _____   V1-5 (Visionary) = _____

H1-5 (Healer) = _____   T1-5 (Teacher) = _____

Scores of 5 or higher might indicate that you have some shadow work to do for that archetype. Did you have any insights from this exercise? What surprised you? What was just as you expected?

***

Did you identify any shadow areas that need work at this time? How have these shadow aspects manifested in your life recently?

***

Look at the items you scored as 2s or 3s. Were your higher shadow scores concentrated in certain archetypes, or rather evenly spread among them? What do you make of the pattern of your scores? How balanced are you (or not) across the archetypes?

Paying Attention to the Inner Critic

Unlike Jung and Bly, David Richo and Angeles Arrien suggested that our shadow characteristics are not always hidden in the unconscious mind. Sometimes they are things that we grudgingly or reluctantly recognize and do not like about ourselves. We consciously try to hide these characteristics from others and we get disappointed or upset with ourselves when we are reminded of them. Most of the time, we ignore or deny them and think we are immune from their influence. We lie to ourselves, thinking, "I've got that under control."

It occurred to me that Angeles' idea of the inner critic would be a good way to identify those forms of shadow that are not as deeply buried in our psyche. For example, perhaps I engaged in some gossip with a colleague, and in this session, I shared some information that another person told me in confidence. This gave me a little thrill, because I felt superior to the person with which I gossiped—I knew something he didn't. But later, I felt guilty. My inner critic started to berate me for breaking this confidence, for getting my kicks out of sharing a secret or a story that was not mine to tell, and for gossiping in general. I try to project a persona of integrity, and this behavior threatens that self-image. Seriously, this is pretty petty behavior, unbecoming of a person of my age.

So, another way to identify shadow is to look at situations that caused your inner critic to jump in with feelings of shame, guilt, or regret. I've developed two ways of assessing the type of shadow identified by the inner critic. This critic is not always bad—it's the ultimate bullshit detector and only bad if we allow it to beat us up. Instead, we can use the energy and spite of the inner critic to identify these shadow qualities and deal with them. Be sure to activate your curiosity for this and all the shadow exercises. As Angeles always said, keep the critic at the gate or on the porch but don't let it trash your house. Over time, we can soften the inner critic and it can become more of a moral compass than a punisher. Think of it as the bouncer at the door who keeps the undesirable elements out of your house!

Inner Critic Practice

Think about the past few months and identify a situation where you felt shame, guilt, or regret about something you did or said. In a nutshell, what was that situation?

***

What was the thought or behavior that caused the inner critic to react? What did you do that your inner critic said was bad?

***

What aspect of shadow might this represent for you? That is, what underlies the shame, guilt, or regret?

***

Is this aspect of shadow a frequent visitor in your life? If so, use exercises later on in this book to acknowledge and befriend it. If it's something new, just note it for now. It may be unique to the situation and not a shadow quality.

Stop/Start Practice

Another way to think about the barely hidden shadow aspects is to make lists that come from the inner critic about your own behavior. The inner critic has been telling you what is wrong with you for a long time—for this exercise, take a few moments to hear what it has to say. Start with what you don't like about yourself by answering this question, giving the inner critic free reign (just for a moment!). Some of us could easily come up with 50 or more items here, but don't let the critic be in control for that long. Just come up with the 3-4 things that first come to mind.

If I could change anything about myself, I would stop:

1.

2.

3.

4.

Consider this list—are any of the things on the list shadow qualities that are not compatible with your image of yourself?

Next, let's go on to solutions. Answer this question:

If I could change anything about myself, I would <u>start</u>:

1.

2.

3.

4.

What is keeping me from starting these behaviors/qualities?

The "stop" list potentially identifies negative shadow qualities whereas the "start" list represents positive shadow characteristics or neglected skill sets, gifts, and talents. The key to moving forward in this exercise using the inner critic is to not indulge the critic's wrath. Use it to productively identify issues in your life but stay in curiosity and self-compassion. Angeles would ask us, "Is your curiosity greater than your criticality?" Are you are keeping the inner critic in check? Notice where criticality got triggered during this exercise.

Re-Dreaming Your Life

Carl Jung (2009) noted that most of us are not living our own lives, but are following the expectations of others. This activity explores areas where you may not be fully living your own life. Re-dreaming and re-creating a life is no easy task. Jung said

> To live oneself means: to be one's own task. Never say that it is a pleasure to live oneself. It will be no joy but a long suffering, since you must become your own creator. If you want to create yourself, then you do not begin with the best and the highest, but with the worst and the deepest (2009, p. 188).

In other words, the hard shadow work comes before the re-dreaming and recreating that ultimately lead to joy. Starting to live our own lives may mean big changes that affect other people—perhaps we are in the wrong relationship, the wrong job, living in the wrong place, not expressing our creativity the way we want to. Other people will be affected. So let's start with the basic question:

Am I living my life or someone else's? What's the evidence of this?

***

Does my work, creative activities, relationships, living circumstances, religious or spiritual practices, parenting, and so on, align with what has heart and meaning for me? Am I using my gifts and talents to their fullest extent? Do I feel alive and present in my own life?

***

If the answer to any of these questions seems to indicate a problem, consider this: What would my ideal life look like?

Using Tasks of the Second Half of Life to Identify Shadow

In *The Second Half of Life* (Arrien, 2005), Angeles proposed that we all have eight gates to traverse; eight developmental tasks that we need to achieve to heal and acquire wisdom for our final days. She also suggests that we are helped along in this endeavor by four major shifts in the way that we perceive the world. The first is a shift from a life driven by ambition, to one of a life seeking to align ourselves and our activities in life with our heart's desire. This drive for meaning requires shadow work. We need to reclaim what we gave up, but that had deep meaning and significance for us, and we need to let go of the mask (persona) that we present to the world and let our authentic selves shine through.

Second, we begin a journey of descent and ascent. The descent is within ourselves to work on the negative shadow characteristics, and the ascent to reclaim the positive shadow and gain in self-awareness and authenticity. Healthy aging depends on doing some deep personal work, or we stay stuck in the superficial world of things and striving.

The third change in perspective involves recognizing the need to integrate our external and internal worlds. The external includes that which can be seen, such as memories, historical events we lived through, turning points and events in our personal lives. The external is the contents of the ego. The internal includes that which is sensed, such as the mystical, spiritual, and soul aspects of ourselves. The internal is part of the shadow. We begin to bring them together when we unearth some of that hidden or buried treasure of the shadow.

The fourth and final shift is one of giving up certainties and dualities (such as good versus evil) and becoming open to paradox and both/and thinking. We can look at all sides of an issue. This is critical to be able to integrate the shadow, as we have to hold paradoxical views of ourselves—I have to acknowledge that both love and hate exist in me and I can hold them both.

This activity concerns the tasks of the eight gates and asks you to ponder what stands in the way of entering this gate. The answer may reveal shadow work to be done at each gate. If you find it hard to generate answers to these questions, consider the four primary aspects of unhealthy ego from David Richo: fear, attachment, control, and entitlement. Chances are, they underlie some of our challenges.

Gate	Task	What stands in the way?
Silver	To invite new experiences into my life: to leave behind the familiar.	
White Picket	To give up/integrate the masks I wore earlier in life (persona). To see beyond my roles and identities, to become my true self.	
Clay	To adjust to a changing physical body and remain a sensual being.	
Black and White	To deepen my relationships by mature forms of love and greater intimacy.	

Gate	Task	What stands in the way?
Rustic	To use creativity to enhance my life, contribute to my community, and leave a legacy.	
Bone	To strip myself of the false self and become my authentic self.	
Natural	To replenish my soul in nature and reflect on life. To reconnect the natural world and my own inner world.	
Gold	To prepare for the final letting go and surrender of my physical body.	

Where do I have second half of life work to do?

Using Projection to Identify Shadows

Jung thought that the shadow appears in dreams and visions, but these are often unreliable and unpredictable events, so they do not make good daily practices. Jung recorded his dreams and spent years analyzing them. See his autobiography, *Memories, Dreams, Reflections* for a fascinating account of his dreams and visions and how many years it took him to fully understand what they meant. Most of us are not that dedicated. If you have the discipline and interest, try keeping a dream journal and see what emerges for you.

Projection, on the other hand, is almost always present in our current lives, and in our past, and we can quite accurately define why we don't like someone, at least on the surface. We project our shadow on others in almost every encounter every day. So this practice uses all of this readily available material from projection to identify shadows.

Projection is a defense mechanism used to protect our egos. Rather than own up to some quality that is not compatible with our persona (the image we project to the outside world), we attribute it to another person. A challenge in using projection to identify shadows, is that our opinions and feelings about other people are not always projections. Sometimes they are accurate observations of patterns of behavior over time. For example, I might dislike a coworker who is highly manipulative and controlling, not because I have those tendencies myself (but probably I do), but because I have witnessed the damage that those behaviors caused in the workplace over an extended period of time. In that case, my opinion may be discernment of a pattern rather than projection. Projections are more likely to happen when we take an instant dislike or distrust of a person because something about them triggered our shadow side, or when our response is disproportionate to what the person said or did. For example, you may say to someone "I don't what it is about that person, but they really bug me." Angeles said that "projections are unclaimed self-perceptions...parts of ourselves that are on their way home, yet are still disowned" (1993, p.96). She also said that projections have an "energetic charge" that distinguish them from factual discernment about the person.

Negative Projections

Think of the past 3-5 years, and list all of the people that you intensely disliked or mistrusted. That is, you feel a negative energy when you think about them. These people may contain the hints of our shadow side. Use the chart below to explore possible shadows, and to identify patterns. Perhaps the underlying shadow is the same for a diverse set of people, suggesting that you have one shadow area that is literally screaming to be seen. Or maybe many different shadow aspects pop up at different times triggered by different people.

Person	What do I dislike/mistrust about this person?	What is the shadow I need to work on?

What surprised you about this exercise, if anything?

***

What challenged you? Did you experience any resistance (e.g., that person is really awful—I'm not projecting!!)? Did you move to rationalizing why you dislike the person for reasons outside of yourself? That might represent another type of defense mechanism (rationalization). Is it possible that the person actually has the negative quality you see in them AND that you are projecting something that you find unacceptable in yourself on them as well?

***

Did you see shadow qualities that seem to ring true for you?

***

Did you see any patterns?

Positive Projections

The next exercise will repeat the projection activity, but this time, think of people that you put on a pedestal—that you think so very highly of that they don't seem quite mortal. These are people that you may admire, feel envious of, or maybe even feel a strong magnetic pull toward. Maybe you idolize or idealize this person. No one is perfect, so perhaps you are projecting a positive quality that is in your shadow onto this person. This person has the quality, but you see it to an exaggerated degree, and overlook the flaws. This might help you to reclaim lost parts of your nature that are positive, such as old life dreams or gifts and talents you gave up to meet someone else's expectations. Angeles always said that if you could see a quality in someone else, you had it within yourself as well. This can be a joyous process as you reclaim all the wonderful things that you might have had to repress or deny about yourself to please others early in your life. Now you can reclaim them! Isn't it ironic that it takes almost as much work to integrate some really great qualities like courage, artistic talents, honesty and authenticity, as it is to acknowledge and integrate the negative ones?

Person	What do I love and most admire about this person?	What is the shadow I need to work on? What is the positive quality that I am not owning?

What insights did you have from this activity?

***

If you identified some positive qualities that you have not been owning, why do you think you relegated them to the shadow? Why do you resist embracing this positive quality of yourself?

For those who worked with Angeles Arrien, I'd like to suggest another exercise on positive projections. Many of us, myself included, idealized Angeles. She was without doubt an exceptional person with a higher level of integrity and authenticity than most. However, she was a mortal being. Perhaps we project some of our own unacknowledged gifts and talents or undeveloped aspects of ourselves on her. Try these questions.

What I admired most about Angeles was

1.

2.

3.

What does this suggest about my own unacknowledged or underdeveloped gifts and talents? How can I channel my inner Angeles?

The Movie Projector

"the shadow is also imagined as a thin gray film rolled up in a can, out of sight, but ready to transfix us with lifelike images thrown onto a giant screen or played on a wife or husband's face" (William Booth in the introduction to Robert Bly's A little book on the shadow)

Many of us love movies—they tell stories in such an impactful way that allows us to love or hate characters, identify with people or situations, or see the world from new perspectives. Stories can humanize people we were taught to distrust or demonize, or they can reinforce hatred and distrust. Stories teach us the ways that people cope with life's challenges. The stories that we are drawn to may offer information that is useful in identifying shadows, and in tracking changes over time. The idea for the activities in this section came from a stimulating conversation with San Francisco therapist Deborah Oak Cooper, who uses this first exercise in her therapy work with couples. Our conversation led me to create the other two exercises related to movies. If you are not a movie buff, you can do these activities with TV shows or books.

A Timeline Approach to the Movies

What movies have you been drawn to over your lifetime? This activity explores the stories that you considered your favorites from childhood on. Have you been drawn to the dark and dangerous stories, the grand romances, the family dramas? Do you favor escapist stories, tales of high imagination, feel good stories? For each time frame, list the movies that you can still recall now with a 1-2 sentence synopsis of the tale, and then speculate about why you liked this movie so much.

Time Frame	Movie(s)	Why I liked these stories
Childhood (up to about 12)		
Adolescence (13-19)		
Young Adult (20-39)		
Midlife (40-59)		
Elder Years (60+)		

Did you see any patterns over the years? Any reasons why you might have been drawn to different types of stories at different ages/stages of life? Were things happening in your life that influenced the type of stories that you needed?

***

If you are in a relationship, and your partner is willing to do this activity, compare your favorite movies and discuss whether you have more similarities or more differences when it comes to the type of movie you are drawn to. Do these differences also extend to other parts of your relationship?

The Shadow Academy Awards

In this exercise, we will look at some of the elements of movies that might illuminate where shadows lie. Do not give this a lot of thought, but just put down the first answer that comes to you. If you repeat this exercise another time, another answer will probably come up.

1. **Best Movie Character**

What character in the movies could I really relate to, or wanted to be like?

What did that character have that I wished I had?

2. **Most Powerful Impact**

What movie made me feel deeply? Why?

Why did I need to feel this way?

3. **Best Movie Villain**

What character was the most evil; the character I loved to hate?

What quality about that person did I react to? Do I recognize this quality in myself?

4. **Best Portrayal of a Different Perspective**

What film helped me to change my beliefs or open my mind about something? Why/How?

5. **Best Genre**

When I am feeling stressed out and need to relax, what kind of film am I most drawn to? (comedy, family drama, sci-fi, action/adventure, kid's movie, true story, documentary, etc.)

What does this choice say about the ways that I self-soothe, or take care of myself?

If this was a productive exercise, think about other categories that you might want to create and explore for yourself.

Stories We Tell

In Sarah Polley's documentary in 2012 of the same name as this activity, she interviewed family members about an event that occurred when she was a child that altered the course of the family. The result was an extraordinarily diverse set of recollections about the "facts" of the event, as well as its repercussions on the family. If so inclined, watch this documentary before you do this exercise, but it is not necessary to being able to do the activity.

Consider a significant event in your life that caused pain or transformed you in some way, whether it happened within the family, at work, at school, or elsewhere. You already know your version of the story, so record it below in nutshell form: that is, the bare bones facts of what happened.

In a nutshell, what happened was:

***

Now consider who the other characters were in the movie version of your event. Construct a different version of the story from each of their perspectives. You may know some of their versions and can record them, but if you do not know their side of the story, make up a plausible version that is different from your own.

***

What did the documentary and your answers to this exercise suggest about the "truth"? Whose version of stories matters most? How do we reconcile an event where we remember circumstances differently from our partners or family members? Where can you see your own shadow emerging in your version of the story, and in other people's versions?

The Arrogant Ego

David Richo, in *How to be an adult in relationships* (2002), suggested that four shadow aspects of the ego often get in the way of developing mature relationships and building intimacy. Each of these "arrogant" traits of the ego, however, are there because they serve a protective function, and each has a positive flip side. The arrogant side contains negative shadow qualities; the healthy ego functions might be conscious, or they might be positive shadows that we do not recognize in ourselves. When we choose the positive qualities, we are more likely to cooperate, apologize and make amends, be ok with making mistakes and learning from them, and have a sense of justice that does not involve revenge.

The table below shows the positive and negative sides of the ego, along with the reason why the negative exists, that is, its function in survival.

The Arrogant Ego	Why it exists	The Healthy Ego
Fear	To assess for danger and make us cautious; to avoid getting hurt.	Loves
Attachment	The capacity to persevere and commit for the long haul. We can become rigid and committed to one particular outcome.	Lets go
Control	The capacity to get things done; efficiency. This can lapse into believing that our way of doing things is the only or best way.	Grants freedom
Entitlement	Self-esteem; standing up for one's rights. Taking care of self. Taken too far, we can become selfish or see ourselves as a victim (martyr).	Sees myself as an equal in the relationship

Think of a situation in a relationship with family or an intimate partner, where one or more of the arrogant ego qualities surfaced for you. How did it affect the relationship? Was there a choice point when you could have accessed the healthy ego? How would the situation have changed if you did?

***

In your past relationships that ended or that you have labeled as "bad" relationships, were you prone to leading with any of the arrogant ego qualities? That is, do you see any patterns in your past relationships related to the arrogant ego?

Mirror Work

Angeles Arrien often used mirrors to identify projections and shadows because of the prevalence of the mirror motif in cultures around the world. In this section, I present two different ways that she used mirrors within groups. In the first, we will turn the mirror to look at ourselves and in the other, we turn it to others. I will talk about how to use them for solitary contemplation instead of in groups. If you ever worked in a group with Angeles, you know how challenging mirror work was—it makes us feel vulnerable. It's ok to go ahead and groan a little before you start this activity.

Looking Inward

In the first mirror practice, look at your own reflection in an actual mirror. Really look at yourself and try to respond to these prompts as honestly as possible. The purpose of the exercise is to deepen self-knowledge.

When I look in the mirror, I see _____.

What I want others to see about me is _____.

What I do not want others to see about me is _____.

Things that trigger my need to look good are _____.

Underneath my need to look good is _____.

If I did not feel a need to look good, I would _____

If done in a group, the other members are witnesses to your work, and do not comment or question your answers to these prompts. This activity might identify what lies beneath some of our common patterns of behavior—the prompt to look underneath the need to look good might identify a shadow aspect of our selves. The final prompt gives the motivation to change. If I did not let this shadow influence my behavior, how much better would my life be? Would I be free of some irrational fears? Let go of attachments? Feel more authentic? Stop hiding my beautiful self?

Looking Outward

The second mirror practice involves our projection onto others. When done in a group, the person takes the mirror and sets it in front of the person who is the object of the projection and describes what has been projected. The types of mirrors that may be relevant to shadow work include:

- **Clear mirror**: this person teaches us about our best self. If I see it in another person, I have it in me as well. I can own it. A clear mirror is a person who captures our imagination and who carries a lot of positive energy for us—someone who ignites the fires of inspiration. So these projections give us a clue to the positive characteristics that we have, but have suppressed or not acknowledged.

- **Neutral mirror**: this is a person I'm so comfortable with that I can just be myself. I need no effort or performance and feel calm and at home with this person. There may not be any projection going on here. Another possibility is that there is something in that other person that allows me to be myself— what is it? Can I capture it so I can feel myself all the time?

- **Smoking mirror**: This person shows where my negative shadow work is; I'm projecting my own stuff on another person. The person who irritates and annoys me can be my best teacher related to shadow work. This person may spark competition, jealousy, or envy (comparison). They bring up "unfinished business" or remind us of someone from our past. Or, most importantly, they possess a quality that we do not want to acknowledge in ourselves.

- **Split mirror**: There are two types. In the fire type of split mirror, this is a person to whom I might be sexually attracted. It's important to acknowledge these to avoid feeding off the sexual energy and sending a mixed message. In the power-type of split mirror, this is the person to whom I give away my power. It's someone that I may have approval needs with, or don't totally trust.

- **No mirror:** This is the person that I have not seen or interacted with. It is important to discern why this person has not registered with me—why have I overlooked this unique individual? This person may represent a part of myself that I have subconsciously rendered invisible or do not want others to see. Who at work, in my extended family, in a spiritual group or other setting, is always there, but with whom I rarely or never interact? What does it say about what I might be avoiding in myself?

When done in groups, this work is very challenging and requires skillful facilitation, because the person sharing their projection and the object of the projection are both rendered vulnerable by the process. But you can do this exercise at home alone, without having to tell the person or group that you are projecting on about your expectations of them. Instead, you can journal about the people who are smoking, neutral, clear, split, or no mirrors for you and dig deeper to identify possible projections. People who are clear or neutral mirrors might be great allies in this work, and you can ask them to witness your progress or participate in the shadow work with you. It might not be necessary to tell others when they are being a mirror for you. Let's face it, most of our coworkers, unless we work in a spiritual retreat center, do not really want us to tell them that they are a "smoking mirror." But for those who are clear and neutral mirrors, you can express your gratitude for having them in your life and tell them what you really like about them. Gratitude is one of the best practices for keeping your heart open and your mind in curiosity. In addition, keep in mind that if someone tells you about a quality that they really like in you, just say thank you. Do not argue that you don't really have this quality! They are giving you a gift.

Think about the people in your life right now who are most important to you, or with whom you interact on a regular basis and identify what kind of mirror that person is for you. Think of co-workers, bosses, family, friends, and acquaintances.

Person	Kind of Mirror	Significance for my own personal work

What did this activity tell you about your shadow or suggest to you about what you might be projecting on other people in your life?

***

Where did you find the greatest energetic charge on your chart? That might signal the greatest possibility of projection.

Visualizing the Shadow

I started this book with an image of myself deliberately putting the sun at my back so that my shadow would be in front of me, where I could see it. In that first photo, it looks like my feet are pinning the shadow down, holding it in place so I could view it more clearly in front of me. Now, I add a photo where my shadow is walking beside me as a companion, a friend. It greets me warmly and can no longer do as much harm. I call it simply, "me and my shadow."

For this exercise, take a walk and contemplate your own shadow. What do you observe about it? What lessons can we learn from observing actual shadows that hint at the metaphorical shadow? Write your insights in your journal.

For the next reflection exercise related to visualizing the shadow, use your creativity to draw, photograph, paint, sculpt, write a poem or a story, create a song, or make a collage that expresses how you see your shadow at this time. After you have done this creative project, answer the following questions. What does your shadow look like? What does it feel like? What aspects of your shadow are fairly clear to you now? What aspects have you glimpsed, but have not worked on yet? Give your creative work a title. As Angeles Arrien always said, if you can name it, you can change it.

David Richo's Frameworks for Integrating Shadow

Angeles often used handouts drawn from the work of psychotherapist David Richo, who showed that the negative and positive qualities are two sides of a coin—if we have a shadow side that we do not like, there is a corresponding positive quality on the other side of it that could be acknowledged and integrated. Richo offers a number of activities to work on shadow. Three of them have been adapted here from *Shadow Dance* (1999).

Practicing Living with Paradoxes

This first activity involves challenging our either/or (dualistic) thinking and embracing that we can be both at the same time. Using the chart below, reflect on actual situations or people in your life where you could practice holding this paradox.

Can I be:	While at the same time:
Angry at someone	Loving toward the same person
Respectful and willing to compromise	Firm in my own values and beliefs
Repulsed by someone's behavior	Caring about the person who did it
Generous	Self-nurturing
Able to see the worst case scenario	Hopeful
Able to take risks	Conscious of safety
Responsible	Spontaneous
Fearful	Capable of taking action
Aware of my faults/shadows	Have high self-esteem

Which of these paradoxes are relatively easy for you to hold? Which ones do you find the most challenging?

Integrating Positive Shadow

For positive qualities that we admire in others, Richo proposed a three-step process for re-integrating the positive aspects of shadow:

> **Affirm** that you have this quality or characteristic. If it's courage, say you are courageous.
>
> **Act** as if you had it. In the next instance when you feel fear, remember that you have courage and act accordingly.
>
> **Announce it**. Tell others that you are making this change toward bringing out your courage. To be witnessed can be a powerful tool toward change; those others can remind you that you are courageous to help reinforce this new behavior.

Now, let's practice. What positive quality have you been suppressing or denying yourself? Say it out loud. You might even consider saying it aloud every day for the next month as a daily affirmation until you start to believe it.

***

What would it look like if you enacted this quality in your daily life? Give a concrete example of how you could employ this characteristic in your life. What would be different in your work, health, relationships, finances, or your own integrity, if you acted out this quality?

***

Who can you announce it to? Who would help hold you accountable in a loving and supportive way?

Integrating the Negative Shadow

For negative qualities like envy, jealousy, judgments, greed, controlling behavior, gossiping, etc., Richo proposed a five-step process of integration. You can do this process repeatedly with different shadow qualities that pop up. Try it with one quality that has emerged as part of your shadow work.

Acknowledge you have all the negative traits that any human can have.

Name one of those traits here:

Allow yourself to hold these parts of yourself so that they can be turned into creativity.

What type of creativity do you think this trait might hold for you?

Admit to yourself and someone else that you have these shadows.

Say it outloud to another person: I have this shadow:_____.

Make amends to those who have been hurt when you denied your shadow or who were harmed by your shadow in any way.

Who has been harmed by your shadow? What would it take to make amends? Are you ready and willing for this step? If not, forgive yourself and commit to continue to work on the shadow until you are ready.

Become aware of the good and positive aspects of the shadow and affirm it as part of yourself.

What would it look like if you affirmed this aspect of yourself? How would you be different?

Robert Bly's Five Stages of Eating Shadow

Now that we have engaged in several practices to identify the shadow, this final exercise involves a slightly more complex process of befriending and integrating the shadow. Bly promoted the idea that there are five stages to reclaiming our shadow aspects. These stages can be explained separately, but in reality they are happening almost simultaneously and to varying degrees for different aspects of shadow. The five stages are listed below, along with an example from my own life.

Stage 1: The projection is sent out and comes to rest on the other person (usually an individual or maybe a group of people).

> For example, I dislike a co-worker whom I judge as being too manipulative and controlling. I have a very strong reaction to this person and everything he says in meetings. I go home at night and tell my partner what a rotten person he is. Although I have always been a non-violent person, I often had a visual image of punching this guy in the nose. In other words, I have a lot of negative energy.

Stage 2: The projection begins to "rattle" or "wobble." The other person displays behaviors or language that are inconsistent with our projection. The projection is unraveling, and we start to get angry with the person for not living up to our projection.

> One day in the midst of my judgments while he was talking, he said something that made sense and that I basically agreed with. I got a glimpse that he is not really all that controlling but offering a rational solution to a work problem.

Stage 3: Attempts to repair the rattling. We try to shore up our projection with rationalizations, excuses, or explanations, but they are not effective. We are disillusioned.

> I've invested a lot of energy into labeling him as despicable and I try to argue myself into disagreeing with him on this issue, but it's getting harder to stay angry with him. He is starting to sound more human to me and more reasonable. He sounded frustrated with the situation that also had me feeling unsettled and unsatisfied. How can that be? I talk to a co-worker who also dislikes this guy and we bond over our dislike, but I have a nagging thought that I'm trying too hard to maintain my

disapproval.

Stage 4: We recognize that the projection diminished us, took away our power. We are not standing in our authentic selves, shadows and all, and this is disturbing.

> I get a glimpse in the mirror and it occurs to me that I wanted to control the same situations that he did, but I just came at it in a different way. Yikes, am I as manipulative and controlling as he is? I want to be seen as flexible, cooperative, and fair, but maybe I am as bad as I thought he was? Was my intense dislike of him because he demonstrated some quality that I cannot acknowledge in myself? Was he actually controlling or was I projecting that explanation on him? I'm still clenching my fist when he talks, but the urge to hit him is lessening. This feeling of aggression toward him is unbecoming and I don't like it.

Stage 5: We eat the shadow (retrieve, reclaim, integrate it back into our being). This is a slow and ongoing process. Winston Churchill once said "I have had to eat many of my own words, and I found the diet very nourishing." This process of eating the shadow helps us to deepen, open, soften, and strengthen (Angeles Arrien—see Eliason, 2016 for more details). We regain energy, spontaneity, and have better capacity for limits and boundaries. In fact, when we digest the shadow, we become lighter beings—the heavy bag we drag behind us has become less dense and heavy!

> I start to examine this issue more carefully. I desperately don't want to be seen as controlling, but often, I rationalize to myself that I see the situation more clearly than my co-workers. I think that my way is better and we should adopt that way. I start to identify that thought (my way is better) as a manifestation of wanting to take control. I recognize that when I am being controlling, it is because I have some fear or some attachment to a particular outcome. The symptom of feeling a need to control is a sign for me that I am too attached. I need to step out for a moment and see what underlies the need to control. What is the fear that is underneath the need to control? That feeling of wanting to take control is now a friend, or at least not an enemy. It is giving me information about my reactions to a situation. I will not stop having urges to control situations, but I can choose to act on them or not. I was also berating myself

because my persona, the image I like to project to the world, is one of a "buddha-like" nature, so that urge to hit him is not who I want to be, and not how I want to be seen. I start to align my thoughts and reactions to him with the ideal person I want to be and feel more compassion.

Now, see if you can analyze a situation with a person that elicited a strong reaction for you. Use one of the projection examples you came up with in the earlier exercises to explore whether you processed the situation and came to befriend the shadow. Or use this as an opportunity to do that integration work now. The table below will help you to work through this. This activity blends Bly's five steps with Angeles Arrien's notion of growth—If I changed in some way, I would have evidence that I deepened, opened, softened, or strengthened in some way. Those are indications that I have successfully integrated the shadow. For example, in my story, I deepened my ability to recognize when I am projecting something on another person. I softened my judgements about the other person and about my own reaction to him. I opened to the idea that I have control issues and that I need to find the fear that underlies it in order to defuse it. Finally, I strengthened in my ability to recognize the control trigger and shift out of the projection before it does too much damage.

What did I project on the other person?	
What were the signs of "wobble" or "rattling" that hinted that this was a projection?	
How did I try to repair the wobble? How did I feel when I noticed the wobble?	
How did this projection diminish me or take away my power? Where did I lose integrity in this projection?	
What value to my life is there if I acknowledge and integrate this shadow? Does it deepen, open, soften, or strengthen me in any way?	

What did you learn about yourself from this activity?

What step was the most challenging for you and why?

***

How did working through these steps affect your attitude toward the object of your projection?

6 CONCLUSIONS

"Now I become myself. It's taken Time, many years and places;
I have been dissolved and shaken, worn other people's faces;
Run madly, as if Time were there, terribly old, crying a warning,
"Hurry, you will be dead before---" (what? Before you reach the morning?
Or the end of the poem is clear? Or love safe in the walled city?)
Now to stand still, to be here, feel my own weight and density!
The black shadow on the paper is my hand; the shadow of a word
As thought shapes the shaper falls heavy on the page, is heard."
May Sarton

We cannot eradicate or merely let go of shadow aspects of ourselves—they are deeply imbedded parts of our selves. They cannot be amputated or exorcised. However, our lives are much improved by paying attention to and befriending our shadow aspects. If we don't do shadow work, we repeat old patterns and continue to project onto others, thus diminishing ourselves and losing integrity. The benefits of shadow work are great. Those individuals who have done much shadow work are visibly different, as Robert Bly noted, "the person who has eaten his shadow spreads calmness." In other words, shadow work builds equanimity, the ability to meet challenges and disturbances in balance in ways that diffuse rather than escalate the situation. Bly also noted:

> The work a person does on his or her shadow results in a condensation, a thickening or a densening of the psyche which is immediately apparent and which results in a feeling of natural authority without the authority being demanding.

I immediately thought of Angeles Arrien when I read this—her wisdom must have entailed a great deal of shadow work, because it was immediately apparent to all in her presence that she had "natural authority." She radiated authenticity and integrity and had a lightness and unique energy about her. Most of us know someone in our lives who is like this, who has befriended their shadow and lives most of their lives in an authentic and genuine place. On the flip side, once you have done some shadow work, it becomes more obvious when other people are allowing their shadow aspects to affect their behavior. If more of us committed to doing this difficult work, we can change the world by our example. One of the greatest illusions in life, Angeles said, was that we could change other people. We can only change ourselves, but when we grow in integrity, this affects everyone that we come into contact with. When others observe the results of befriending the shadow on our lives, they may be motivated or inspired to change as well. There is always a ripple effect out onto our entire social networks when we act with more integrity. We will never be perfect, because the shadow is never completely integrated, but we can be more genuine and authentic when we acknowledge that fact.

Maybe your experience with shadow work is one of grasping in the darkness—you may have had inklings of a shadow lurking out of sight, but it did not yet emerge into your conscious mind. Maybe you were walking into the sun, so that the shadow was behind you, out of sight. That's ok, too. Shadow work is the work of a lifetime. That hidden shadow is not going anywhere—it will emerge in more obvious ways in the future. You can rest assured that it won't go away until you deal with it! Jung said, "what we resist, persists."

Nor is your bag of shadows like Pandora's box. It may be scary to open it and peer inside, but your own survival and well-being lies in doing just that. You will not be releasing evil into the world—in fact, you will be doing the opposite. Identifying your shadow helps you with containment. So in the meantime, think of your shadow as that place in the shade on a hot day--a metaphorically pleasant place to lie on your blanket or swing in your hammock, slow down to nature's rhythm, out of the glaring hot light of the summer sun to open the long bag and contemplate the shadows inside. It may make a nourishing picnic lunch.

The end result will not be a perfect life, nirvana, or the solution to every problem you encounter. Parker Palmer noted "Wholeness does not mean perfection—it means embracing brokenness as an integral part of life." You will not transform into the Dalai Lama immediately (but even his holiness has broken parts, no doubt). That embracing of the dualism whole and broken is one of the main outcomes of shadow work. You can be broken and still achieve wholeness. As Angeles always used to point out, we are strongest at the healed broken places.

For several months before I wrote this book, I was coming home from work exhausted, sometimes napping in the late afternoon but still feeling mentally drained upon waking. I was spending a lot of time binge-watching Netflix or reading Facebook posts because I had no energy for more "productive" activities. I was feeling a vague restlessness and my inner critic was brow-beating me a bit for not doing something more meaningful with my time. Then all of a sudden one day when taking a beach walk, I noticed my shadow stretched out ahead of me. It was dark and looming, like I was walking toward it. The idea came to me that writing about the shadow was going to be my annual integration project. After four years of saying that I needed to do shadow work, now I was ready to embark on it. I began to read and write and in the course of three evenings, finished a first draft outline. I was awake, alert, and completely engaged in the process.

The evening I finished the draft, I felt more energized than I had felt in months. Even though I only tangentially addressed my own shadow work in the process of writing about it, I felt I had laid out the blue print for the work ahead of me. Glimpses of shadow were emerging as I worked on describing the practices. Angeles always suggested that at least once a year, we consider what has opened, deepened, strengthened, and softened in our nature. Writing about shadow work had created the opening, doing the actual practices was the grist for the deepening work, the integration of shadow would strengthen my authentic self, and I would ascend from the process a bit softer and more gentle with myself and others.

As you continue with your shadow work, consider what kinds of daily practices would help you to soften, deepen, strengthen, and open your own authentic nature. The work is made easier if you keep your curiosity stronger than your criticality and keep your heart open. Shadow work is the work of a lifetime, with ups and downs, but with incredible rewards. The more shadow work you do, the more likely that your ideal self will align with your actual self, and you will live in greater integrity. Consider continuing to write in a shadow journal and lay out your intentions for future work. You can track your progress and practice "eating the shadow." Sometimes it will taste like a bitter pill, and other times it will be sweet and juicy. Bon Appetit!

7 WORKS CITED

Angeles Arrien (1993). *The Four Fold Way: Walking the paths of the Warrior, Teacher, Healer and Visionary.* San Francisco: HarperSanFrancisco.

Angeles Arrien (2005). *The Second Half of Life: Opening the Eight Gates of Wisdom.* Boulder, CO: Sounds True.

Robert Bly (1988). *The Little Book of the Shadow.* NY: HarperCollins.

Mickey Eliason (2016). *Reflecting on the Teachings of Angeles Arrien.* Amazon Createspace.

Katie and Gay Hendricks (2018). *The Surprising Reason You Become Deeply Upset with Your Partner.* Blog: www.heartsintrueharmony.com.

Robert Johnson (1991). *Owning Your Own Shadow: Understanding the Dark Side of the Psyche.* NY: HarperCollins.

Carl Jung (1961). *Memories, Dreams, Reflections.* New York: Vintage.

Carl Jung (1964). *Man and His Symbols.* London: Albus Books.

Carl Jung (1990). *The Undiscovered Self.* Princeton, NJ: Princeton University Press.

Carl Jung (2009). *The Red Book.* New York: Norton Press.

Parker Palmer (2018). On The Brink of Everything: Grace, Gravity, and Getting Old. Oakland, CA: Berrett-Koehler Publishers.

David Richo (1999). *Shadow Dance. Liberating the power and creativity of your dark side.* Boston, MA: Shambala Press.

David Richo (2002). *How To Be An Adult in Relationships.* Boston: Shambala Press.

Von Franz, Marie Louise (1997). *Archetypal Patterns in Fairy Tales.* Toronto, Canada: Inner City Books.

Connie Zweig and Steve Wolf (1997). *Romancing the Shadow: A Guide to Soul Work for a Vital, Authentic Life.* NY: Ballantine.

ABOUT THE AUTHOR

Mickey Eliason was born and raised in Iowa, and became a San Franciscan when she was in her 50s. She is an academic by day and fanatic consumer of personal growth activities by night. Much of her nonacademic work has focused on issues raised in her work with Angeles Arrien, culminating in books based on Angeles' teaching (*Reflections on the Teaching of Angeles Arrien*), the role of nature in personal and spiritual growth (*Blessings from the Beach*, and *My Life as a Tree*), and the concept of silence (*The Bittersweet Territory of Silence*, *forthcoming*). She also has one book of lesbian humor (*The Dyke Dykignostic Manual*). All of these books are available on Amazon. She is also a budding novelist, although that bud has not yet opened. Hopefully some aspect of shadow work will tap into the creative potential needed for that endeavor. Finally, in looking through childhood photos, this gun control advocate, who really believes that no child should be taught that guns are toys, was appalled to find herself holding a pistol at age 2. This may be the first shadow that she tackles in her own personal work!

Made in the USA
Coppell, TX
10 September 2020